MW00895366

Chocks Away

Achieving freedom from the 9 to 5

James McBrearty

Published 2010

© 2010 by James McBrearty.

ISBN10   1-84914-062-6
ISBN13   978-1-84914-062-1

All rights reserved. No part of this publication may be reproduced, stored in a retrieval system, or transmitted in any form or by any means, electronic, mechanical, photocopying, recording or otherwise, without the prior permission of the author.

BNI® and Givers Gain® are registered trademarks of BNI

"Know me, Like me, Follow me" Copyright © The Ecademy Ltd. 2009 - 2010

"Open, Random, Supportive" Copyright © The Ecademy Ltd. 2009 - 2010

"ORS" Copyright © The Ecademy Ltd. 2009 - 2010

"Closed, Selective, Controlling" Copyright © The Ecademy Ltd. 2009 - 2010

"CSC" Copyright © The Ecademy Ltd. 2009 - 2010

Front cover image © Julian Slaughter - Fotolia.com

Index

Foreword

By Penny Power, the founder of Ecademy:

I first met James at an Ecademy local group meeting and was drawn to him because he clearly understood his unique contribution as a Tax Specialist and how to market himself online.

He has created a fantastic online presence while maintaining the power of the offline through attending Ecademy and BNI meetings. Very often the power of the online world is how it enables you to meet and keep in touch with people offline too.

James is likeable, bright, calm and friendly. He believes in friendship and supporting others. For that reason he is often re-quoted and retweeted. His content in blogs is solid, inspiring and provides tips that apply to many of us.

James is the most perfect example of a man who owns a traditional business and has learned to adapt to a new world; a world of open sharing, random connections and supportive actions and communication.

Introduction

So, you're thinking about becoming self employed or maybe you are in the early stages and have discovered things aren't going exactly as you thought they would?

Rather than struggle along trying to find things out yourself, as many people do, why not get a head start on your competition?

First, here's the bad news:
In the past many people running successful small sole trader businesses didn't always share what had and hadn't worked for them. They found things to be such a struggle when they started their own business and believed keeping this knowledge to themselves was actually protecting their business.

Indeed, there is a high failure rate for new businesses as so many people don't understand the hidden elements involved in the start up phase.

Running a business is not just the job you *want to do* it's the other jobs that you *have to do* as part of being a business owner. It's these that many people don't allow for.

As Michael Gerber says in his book 'the E-myth revisited', as a self employed business owner you actually now have three jobs - the employee, the manager, and the CEO. Many people make the mistake and think that they just need to be the employee only when working for themselves.

Another thing to realise is the hours you will need to put in, particularly in the early years, as these will be far in excess of those needed when you were an employee working for someone else.

Taking Mr Gerber's example, if you were doing these three roles full time then instead of the eight hour day you may be familiar with you now need to work a twenty four hour day, which doesn't leave much time for anything else! It's simply not possible to work any harder, so instead you need to work smarter.

Now, here's the good news:
We are seeing massive changes in the way business is being done.

Penny Power, the founder of Ecademy, describes this as the world rebooting itself and the emergence of the digital economy. So many people, when you tell them about the opportunities available right now in the digital economy, just reply 'I don't have time for that, I'm too busy working.'

Here's the interesting fact, the social media SAVES time when used correctly and it should be a key part of your business strategy.

Using it correctly is the important part to grasp, without direction it can indeed use up huge amounts of time with little or no business result. Another piece of good news - there are experts in the field that can help you, you only need to seek their guidance and be open to the changes that are happening now in the digital economy.

Three years ago I hadn't even heard of using online networking and the opportunities it presented. It's a skill I've developed over that time and it's a skill that *you can develop too.* Similarly, the world of offline networking is linked with this - they are not mutually exclusive of one another and, when combined, are a powerful force.

It is well worth finding out how to tap into these resources, and avoiding the mistakes so commonly made by the self employed business person.

In this book I will share my journey and how I discovered these changes and communities. I'll give you a tour of my development in the early stages of the changing business world both offline and online – and how you can benefit from this shift in your own business.

I have a somewhat unique perspective, as creating and growing a successful self employed business from scratch is something I've already done myself with taxhelp.uk.com, rather than the more usual route of starting a practice through taking over an existing business. I know exactly what it's like to be a self employed sole trader as I've done it myself.

Yes, I've made some mistakes along the way - *but you don't have to unless you want the experience.* I'm going to share these so that you can avoid them.

As a taste of what's possible, these changes mean that now you have the same marketing influence available as the major corporations once did. Now budget is no longer the critical factor in success.

Exciting times...

Acknowledgements

I would like to thank the following people, who have helped me on my journey and who I personally recommend. I owe much of what I know to them and the help they have given me in developing my knowledge, which they have freely shared:

Penny & Thomas Power
The founder and the chairman of Ecademy - a social network where business happens. Ecademy was my first venture into the world of social networking for business and it is the network where I built up my knowledge.
It's not just an online network; through local group meetings I've also met many people who are embracing the new supportive nature of business.
I also discovered my Core Process with Thomas, "Achieving Freedom", and it has given me a greater focus. It's also included in the title of this book as I want to help others achieve their own freedom.
www.ecademy.com

Ivan Misner
Dr Misner is the founder of BNI, the world's number one business referral organisation. Through BNI I have been able to develop my presentation skills. From initially speaking to only a few people at my local BNI meeting I am now comfortable presenting to groups of over a hundred, and have also presented internationally too.
As well as being a member of BNI in my local chapter I am also a BNI Assistant Director and now able to help others on their own journey too by training BNI members, both in the UK and internationally.
www.bni.com

Tom Evans

Tom specialises in helping authors remove writer's blocks and find their Creative Muse. He is also an expert at Digital Publishing. His suggestions and attention to detail have both widened this book's scope and deepened its applicability.

www.thebookwright.com

Anthony Robbins

I discovered Tony during my search for improvement when growing my business, and have learnt a lot about myself through his audio programmes and his UPW seminars.

www.tonyrobbins.com

Vanessa Warwick & Nick Tadd

They are experts both in the field of property and social media and run their own website to help landlords share any issues they may have in business.

As well as running property networking events, they also share their knowledge of the changes due to the digital economy.

The videos I have on my website were shot by Nick and Vanessa, as they both also have extensive experience in the TV industry, and are able to use this to help businesses generate more clients.

www.socialmediagraffiti.com
www.propertytribes.ning.com

I would also like to thank Ces & Jay Loftus and Richard White, who have all helped me immensely.

Pilot report

*As a pilot it's important to know exactly **where you are** and **where you are going** ...*

Where am I now?

I am the owner of a successful business, taxhelp.uk.com Ltd, which specialises in helping self employed people pay less tax and avoid fines.

By combining affordable fixed fees and a personal service, taxhelp.uk.com has experienced significant growth in both turnover and profit each year, despite the financial conditions of the market.

We have several hundred clients, mostly located in the Surrey area and the reason I specialise in helping self employed people is that I have the experience of starting and growing a business myself, after leaving the corporate world.

Many of our clients have themselves left the corporate world and as well as the compliance side of the business I can help them with growth and networking for their business as it's something I have done myself.

As well as running my business, I am also an Assistant Director for BNI, the world's largest business referral network. My role with BNI involves me travelling internationally and delivering BNI training to members, to audiences in excess of one hundred people as well as individually to smaller groups and on a one to one basis.

As well as offline, I network extensively online and am known as 'the twittering tax man' there, and also regularly run a presentation on 'Social Networking for Business' to various networking groups to share my experiences.

My business is registered in practice with the Association of Taxation Technicians (ATT), who are the leading professional body for those providing tax compliance services and related activities in the UK.

I also serve on the 'Member & Student Services' Committee of the ATT and regularly attend their meetings at their head office in London. In September 2010 I presented to the committee, on social networking. This was initially scheduled to be for ten minutes however we were still debating the issues an hour later, as there are so many opportunities.

I am the author of several briefing papers on tax and how it applies to the self employed and I have also lectured on tax and accounts to a class of entrepreneurs at St Mary's University, Twickenham.

I regularly post online through blogs and comments, and am also featured in Penny Powers' book 'Know me, Like me, Follow me.'

Outside of the office, I am a private pilot and hold both European and American licences. I have built up over three hundred and fifty hours in my logbook to date internationally, and qualified to fly on instruments in clouds and bad weather, as well as at night. I have so far flown twenty five different types of aircraft, ranging from very light two seat aircraft up to twin engine aircraft costing in excess of four hundred thousand pounds. I've even be lucky enough to fly several multimillion pound airline flight simulators.

Where is my destination?
The company is achieving significant growth year on year, *in a recession*, proving that the model is successful and there is a demand for the service.

There is a limit to how many people we can help though, and there is also a national market for our service that we haven't pursued yet.

Therefore my next step will be to franchise the business, and I am planning to do this within the next three to five years.

Franchising will bring a different set of opportunities, as I then move from running the business to managing the franchise.

With my experience in growing the business personally, and my networking skills developed both online and offline I am well positioned to help the franchisees. I have already been through exactly the same situations they will be going through as new business owners, as well as those of many of their clients.

Our projections are showing that within five years of launching the franchise, as well as being able to help thousands of people pay less tax and avoid fines and also helping our franchisees to achieve their own freedom, we will be looking at a company with an annual profit into seven figures...

So, how did I get here?

Under radar control

*When you are flying under air traffic control, **they** are making the decisions as to where you fly, to fit in with **their** own goals ...*

Like many people, when I started in the business world I worked for other people as an employee.

I had always had an interest in IT and finance so my initial career plan was to become a chartered accountant and to then use the qualification working within the finance field. The qualification also opens many different opportunities in the business world, not limited to just becoming a pure accountant. Indeed, many CEO's of top companies are also accountants.

There are several ways to qualify as an accountant. Many people start a training contract with a firm as a junior and complete their training with one employer. The route I chose was not to be tied to one firm and was to instead study while working full time, as this enabled me to develop the practical experience in a variety of environments, not limited to just within a practice.

My first role was in the finance department for a large multinational retail business, based at their head office in London. This was an interesting role as I came into contact with other people who were also in the process of taking their initial accountancy exams so it was good to be able to chat with them about the exams whilst also learning about the profession.

I stayed with the firm for a year and learnt a fair amount about working in industry.

A role then became available in a Surrey firm of independent financial advisers, working in their personal tax department. The firm had around 30 staff so there was a greater exposure to the business than with the international firm where I had a smaller role in the overall scheme of things. Being a locally based firm also meant that I was saving a significant amount of time each week commuting, which gave me more time for my studies.

It was a serious commitment studying for the accountancy qualification while working full time. At times it was somewhat difficult having to spend my evenings and weekends studying, but it went well and, as I was placing in the top twenty percent of accountancy students worldwide with my exam results. All in all though, I was pleased with my progress and my *flight plan*.

At this time personal computers were just being introduced into offices for business use, replacing typewriters for the secretaries and also replacing mainframe terminals for other roles. I was lucky that I had always had an interest in computers and had several of the first home computers myself. In addition to my tax role, I also took on the systems manager role for the firm and then had the responsibility for introducing PC's, a network to connect them together and dealing with IT support. This was in the early days of computing and the level of connectivity and performance that we take for granted now wasn't always the norm.

Over a period of nine years, I worked my way up through the tax department. Having started as an adviser, I progressed to the assistant manager and then to the role of tax manager, running the department and managing the department staff. It was an interesting time and I learnt a lot about tax as well as the duties of being a manager.

The firm was then taken over and would be relocating to central London, which would then involve a round trip commute of at least three hours a day - assuming everything ran on time. I looked for a more local role in the tax and accountancy field.

I have always been surprised by the number of people that regularly commute and spend two to three hours a day on their round trip. What they may not realise is that over a five day week they are actually losing between one and two full days worth of work *every week*! Another way of thinking about this is if you add the commuting time to the hours worked for the salary given you actually find that your hourly earnings aren't any more than with a local role. And with the costs of commuting to add on top, suddenly what you thought was a higher salary is actually *less*.

Whilst I had completed most of the accountancy exams by that time, qualifying as an accountant also requires practical experience of many different areas as well, and to have these signed off during training.

So, for the next couple of years I pursued various short term assignments, both in industry and accountancy practices in order to meet these practical requirements. This was to turn out to be very useful experience and knowledge of the market later on.

However, I then hit a spot of turbulence.

I'd worked hard and completed all the practical experience requirements and all the exams apart from the final stage;

however once I completed the final stage I wouldn't be able to practice as a chartered accountant without a practising certificate. The usual way to get one of these is by staying with your training firm for a year after qualification and then taking the examination, however I had pursued a non-traditional route by working for various firms.

Whilst on average people in the UK may change employers every five years or so, with this time span decreasing, I found that within practice the number of years people spent working for the same employer tended to be much higher than this.

There was a huge difficulty in trying to find a firm willing to take me on for the final stage leading to the practising certificate - perhaps they might be worried that I would leave and start up in competition against them after qualifying? So since I took off, air traffic control had changed the rules and I wasn't clear to land anywhere.

After much thought I set another course by switching sideways to a tax qualification, and convert my accountancy experience to date into a different qualification rather than the pure chartered route I was initially aiming for. This gave me a dual qualification in both tax and accounts and opened up more possibilities as I would be able to practise on the basis of my tax qualification, which is now actually the leading qualification for those working in the tax field. It was as if I'd somehow taken off with a single engine and acquired another on route without coming in to land!

A role in industry then became available for an international chemical firm, locally based again, and ideal as I could concentrate on what I really enjoyed, which was giving personal tax advice. The role was a complete change from the world of the accountancy practices and had a very relaxed environment overall which included such benefits as flexitime and the business casual dress code.

The role was extremely varied, one week I could be working with HR on the company's employee benefit packages and the next meeting with the finance directors of their local offices throughout the UK, advising them on current employee tax issues.

There was some business travel involved, both throughout the UK and to the head office in Switzerland, however as it was a large firm they had good policies in place for their business travel so these trips were enjoyable as well and didn't cause any problems for me.

Their UK office was based on the outskirts of the town in Surrey so my daily lunchtimes now usually involved relaxing walks in the country. As well as this, the benefits package was very good and also included membership of one of the last final salary pension schemes.

Things were going really well, certainly the environment was the best I had experienced and I really enjoyed the varied responsibilities of the role combined with the great overall package.

However the industry was changing and consolidating and after I had been there three years I was called into a meeting one cold January morning, to be told that I was being made redundant. More turbulence just when I wasn't expecting it.

This was a complete shock, I had been in a role I enjoyed and had become very comfortable in. I hadn't planned to leave and was intending to stay with the firm for many years.

However, as the song goes, *you can't always get what you want, but sometimes you get what you need.*

This was the real start of my journey.

Filing a flight plan

Before a flight, you need to decide what your destination is going to be so that you can land where you are aiming

...

I was also very fortunate in that, due to my time with the firm and its size, I had a generous redundancy package which gave me several months 'gardening leave' and a budget for retraining.

I had time to think about what I really wanted, a blank sheet of paper without any restrictions, and decided that working for myself was my goal.

Being my own boss meant that redundancy wouldn't be an issue again and I would be responsible for my own future. There are financial benefits too when it's your own business as the income achievable is much higher than that when being an employee, as well as the flexibility it opens with holidays and working hours to suit your own schedule.

I didn't know how to achieve this at the time, but I knew it was what I wanted to do.

I'd also qualified for a private pilot's licence three years earlier, which was a lifetime goal of mine. I had always wanted to fly since I had been a young boy but was deterred as I wear glasses and believed that you had to have perfect eyesight in order to be a pilot.

Qualifying as a private pilot involved several challenges. I'd been somewhat less than fit earlier in life, so getting in shape and passing the medical was the first challenge I overcame.

After that there were seven written exams to complete, covering the subjects of: Air Law and Operational Procedures, Aircraft General and Principles of Flight, Flight Performance and Planning, Human Performance and Limitations, Meteorology, Navigation and Radio Navigation, and Radio Telephony Communications. Just reading this list is enough to put anyone off even trying!

As well as the written examinations, I also had to complete the flying expcricncc too, which is a minimum of forty hours followed by two flight tests with an examiner - the navigational flight test and the general handling flight test.

Flight training in the UK can be a frustrating experience sometimes due to our somewhat unique and changeable weather. There is also the cost element to consider as flying lessons cost more than just hiring a plane once you have the licence, as you are paying for the instructor too.

Generally many people in the UK complete their training over a year, but overall it took me five years to complete the requirements. I had three tries with different flight schools before I settled into the final one that I qualified with. Working full time also meant that, as for many pilots, my flying was almost always restricted to weekends only.

Initially I heard about a private flying club that had a small office at Biggin Hill airfield, so I did a few hours training with them. It was a fairly long drive for me to get there though and with the airfield being based on a hill sometimes the weather was no good there, despite being ok where I lived. I had several trips there only to find that there was no flying and I had to drive straight back home. After a few of these I lost my enthusiasm for the club and took a break.

After a while my thoughts returned to flying again and this time I went to the closest airfield to me, which was Fairoaks near Woking in Surrey. I completed my first solo flight there in a Piper PA28 warrior, however being based near to London the costs were fairly expensive and I had to take a break after getting as far as this.

A couple of years later, whilst I was performing short term assignments for various firms, it meant that I had the time between these to train midweek as well as at weekends and I found a school at Redhill that was offering flying training at a low cost.

It was again a fair amount of travel but the location was better, being just a few miles up the road from London Gatwick international airport. I felt comfortable there and was able to complete my training fairly quickly and finally qualified as a private pilot in August 2000.

Flying has been an interest of mine for a long time and I'm sure growing up with the images of pilots in movies and on TV was a big influence. Even seeing Charlton Heston in the 'Airport' movies, inspired me to dream about what to do after being made redundant. I had the idea at the time of working nine months of the year doing tax returns and accounts and spending three months of the year flying business jets as a commercial pilot. This would give me a secure financial backing against possible downturns in the aviation industry, as well as allowing me to fly varied routes in the three months when the personal tax side of the business is traditionally quieter.

Back in early September 2001 I had travelled to the USA to attend a two day course in Denver, Colorado to find out just what it was like to be an airline pilot.

The Airline Transport Orientation Program (ATOP) was a course that ran over a weekend at a major airlines flight training facility in the USA and involved a condensed course on the Boeing 737-200. This involved all the training on the operation of its different systems and the normal flight procedures that an airline pilot goes through on a typical flight.

The first day was taken up with the basic systems training and also practicing drills in a cockpit simulator. On day two we actually flew the multimillion pound full motion airline simulator - with a couple of approaches using the instrument landing system and also the occasional emergency thrown in by our simulator instructor.

It was satisfying that at the end of the course we were able to start a 'cold & dark' Boeing airliner and be able to take off, fly it and then land it too.

Whilst there I also took an additional course option that was available and which qualified me to fly pressurised aircraft, the FAA 'high altitude endorsement.' This involved extra ground training as well as a check flight in the simulator, where we simulated a depressurisation and a rapid descent down to level that didn't require oxygen.

There were several of us on the course and it gave us a real introduction into the world of airline flying and what was involved. We all came from different backgrounds and there was a mixture of ages too. People there ranged from a college student to an already qualified commercial pilot on propeller aircraft and to someone nearing early retirement and considering a career change.

After returning to the UK though the following week was when the 9/11 attacks happened.

It was a real blow and I remember being hit by it quite hard. Only a few days before I had been training alongside crew in Denver that may have actually been flying that day.

Suddenly being able to fly an airliner (even though it was in a limited capacity) wasn't something that you openly shared.

This also put a hold on any ideas of following through on my commercial ambitions at the time, due to the industry then going through a major period of change.

The course did mean that later, while considering my options in redundancy, I had the background knowledge to know what the realities were like. However I hit another stumbling block here with the UK professional pilots qualifications as I discovered that there is a limit to the strength of your glasses prescription for the initial grant of an airline pilots medical.

This is a rather unusual rule as I discovered that there is no such restriction for glasses strength with an American airline pilots medical.

In a rather roundabout way I would still be able to qualify for a UK professional licence if I did the American one first and then converted my American licence to a UK one! I found out that the higher eyesight limit in the UK does not apply if you already have a professional licence from another country and are just converting it.

Many aircraft operated in Europe are actually registered in America for many reasons. So as long as the aircraft I was flying had an American registration number on the side, I could fly it professionally on my American licence and medical.

This whole debacle is typical of aviation red tape; however at least I had a way round it.

My retraining budget covered training towards a commercial pilot's licence and in less than a month I had passed the highest American medical, which covers airline pilots.

I also committed myself to the flying training and over a period of less than one month I flew on most days, and sometimes several times in a day.

The result at the end of an intense month was that I had now passed the UK IMC rating; this is a rating for private pilots that qualifies you to fly an aeroplane inside clouds and in bad weather when the visibility is much lower than with a standard pilots licence. You also learn how to use the same navigation and instrument landing systems that commercial airliners do, so that apart from takeoff and landing you can fly the whole flight without being able to see anything outside the windows.

Whilst the IMC rating is valid for UK private pilots only, the instrument hours I accumulated for this also counted towards the experience requirements for the grant of my American full instrument rating. The American instrument rating would train me to a greater standard and also allow me to fly alongside commercial planes in restricted airspace, such as at London Heathrow or Gatwick.

As well as qualifying for the IMC rating, I also completed training and was checked out on what are termed 'complex' planes. Generally most private planes have wheels that are fixed in position and a simple fixed pitch propeller. As you venture onto more advanced aircraft, you find that these usually have retractable undercarriage and propellers that can be adjusted in the air to bring better cruising performance (similar to changing gears in a car.)

On top of this, at the same time I also completed my night rating. A standard UK private pilot's licence allows you to fly during the day and up to half an hour before or after sunset before it is officially classed as being night time.

I completed additional training so that I could fly during the night hours, navigating and landing - both with and without the landing light, in case it failed when you were flying. Landing without a landing light is actually fairly straightforward as you can judge your height from the position of the runway edge lighting in your peripheral vision.

Flying at night is a great experience, the winds are generally calmer and it gives you another perspective on towns and cities when you can see them at night. Whenever I am on a commercial flight at night I always take a window seat and am surprised how many people pull down the blind and never look outside - missing such a great view.

With everything I had now done, this took my total experience up to the level that is required to apply to complete the final training for an American commercial pilot's licence, which I could do within two to three weeks – most easily by travelling to the USA as examiners are more freely available and the costs are much lower.

It was intense time but I relished the challenges and as well as flying almost every day there was the ground training to complete and also the written instrument exam, followed by the instrument flight test which involved navigating and flying the landing approach at airports without being able to see out the window.

During training and on the examination flight you can't guarantee bad weather so to account for this pilots wear a hood on their head. Basically a big baseball cap that lets you look in front of you at the instruments but it blocks your view out of the windows. Of course whilst you are simulating instrument flight the instructor is maintaining a good look out for other planes and you also have radar coverage helping you as well.

The training is something that I really enjoyed, and it is something I plan to complete when time and finances allow, as with over three hundred and fifty hours now I have far exceeded the two hundred and fifty hour requirement for the basic American commercial pilot's licence.

After that, things do get fairly expensive though - there is then a multi-engine rating and the full American instrument rating to add on. Also, flying larger planes is more expensive than the typical single engine trainers you use in the early stages of qualification; and again there are also more exams and studying too.

The top qualification is an Airline Transport Pilots Licence (ATPL), which also involves many more hours of flying experience and exams. That's not the end, as the licence on its own won't let you fly a jet. For that you need a type rating, which is training so that you are cleared to operate that specific model of aircraft. The total cost for a type rating can run to around twenty thousand pounds depending on the complexity of the aircraft you intend to fly.

In explaining what it's like to be a pilot, John Magee said it best in his poem 'High Flight' written in 1941:

"Oh! I have slipped the surly bonds of Earth and danced the skies on laughter-silvered wings;

Sunward I've climbed, and joined the tumbling mirth of sun-split clouds, and done a hundred things you have not dreamed of—wheeled and soared and swung high in the sunlit silence.

Hov'ring there, I've chased the shouting wind along, and flung my eager craft through footless halls of air....

Up, up the long, delirious, burning blue I've topped the wind-swept heights with easy grace where never lark nor even eagle flew

And, while with silent lifting mind I've trod the high untrespassed sanctity of space, put out my hand, and touched the face of God."

Slipping the surly bonds

During the takeoff roll in a jet there is a point of no return when you are committed to takeoff, no matter what ...

I knew now that self employment was something I wanted to do, particularly as once established it would provide the funding and flexibility for me to complete my commercial pilot's licence. I felt though that I didn't have the experiences I needed at that point to start my own business, so when a role running the tax department for a local accountancy practice came up I took this instead.

I'm sorry, that last paragraph is BS - what stopped me from leaving the employed world and becoming self employed was fear, as it's quite a shock to leave the corporate world and start again if it is all you have ever known. I simply wasn't ready for takeoff.

[By the way, I was to learn later that BS just stands for 'Belief System', thanks to Tony Robbins.]

It was a good experience running the tax department for a local accountancy practice and I initially enjoyed the challenges. There had been some issues with the previous manager and when I started I turned around a loss making department in less than nine months and also instigated reporting and tracking systems that hadn't existed before, a particular skill of mine from my IT background.

I was managing two staff and they had a good mix of backgrounds so I could learn more about their own experiences in practice. One of the staff had also run her own business before selling her clients to the practice and then staying for a few months to help with the transfer, so it was good to be able to discuss self employment with her as she had the experience of doing it herself, although on a very small scale.

I came into regular contact with local small business owners over a period of a couple of years and got to know the typical problems and worries that are common to most people, which was invaluable knowledge for later.

The initial challenges were exciting and I enjoyed working there however my goal of becoming self employed had slipped and it was actually fortunate that, following a change in business ownership, the management style of the firm changed.

This was something I had come across a few times when contracting in various firms, the difference between what Thomas Power explains as Closed Selective and Controlling (CSC) and Open Random and Supportive (ORS.)

People work better in environments that suit them and I had discovered that the ORS environment was very much suited to me personally - which is ideal as with the shift occurring in business now ORS environments will emerge to be more common, whereas is the past CSC was the norm in many of the more traditional professions.

In industry the environment I experienced had been ORS - I had a task and a deadline and it was up to me to plan to achieve the goal, calling on other staff members for collaboration if needed and there was also flexible working available, a relaxed attitude, and a supportive environment. As long as the goals were reached in the timescale planned for, there was freedom in how you achieved this.

The opposite of this is the CSC environment I had already experienced occasionally while contracting - very much less freedom and micromanaging staff including things such as timesheets to account for every minute of the day.

For me, the CSC nature of the firm was increasingly beginning to drag and also remind me of what I really wanted to do before I took the job.

Whilst on holiday from the practice, I was able to take the time one day for a walk in the woods and to consider my options there with no distractions. Walking is another hobby of mine and I enjoy the time it gives me to clear my mind and focus on my thoughts. Incidentally, when working on this book, I was fortunate to spend some time walking with The Bookwright and his dogs - the best friends a writer could wish for.

I spent the day with Ray Mears, walking through the woods in Sussex on one of his bushcraft courses. Whilst there I was also privileged to see him make his first fire of the year, which he did by just rubbing two sticks together.

In case you haven't heard of him, Ray Mears is a famous British woodsman, instructor, author and TV presenter. He has recorded many different programmes covering the outdoors which can regularly be seen on TV.

After my day with Ray the seeds had been planted; I knew I had to leave at some point in the near future.

Going back to the office after that experience was somewhat deflating to say the least, returning to the CSC environment after the freedom I had experienced, although only briefly.

I expect there are a lot of people in the same situation I found myself in - a good regular income but not enjoying their time, wanting more and unsure of exactly what to do next. We feel shackled by gravity to the Earth with the chocks preventing our wheels from even moving.

This was a difficult time and I wrestled with what to do for several months, considering the implications of leaving to start up on my own - how would I start and grow the business and financially what where the implications of leaving?

The 'sensible' thing for many people might be to stay in a secure job and take a regular income but I couldn't accept that. I wanted more and it had got to a point where I had had enough and finally took the decision to make the leap and handed in my notice.

Handing in my notice felt good and I realised at that point I had waited too long and should have done it several months before. I knew there was a great adventure awaiting me, which wasn't bounded by the CSC rules I had been experiencing, and I was excited about the possibilities. The chocks were away!

You get to a point where you have to make the decision and act, one I think is said well by a quote that inspired me:

"Now is the time to believe in ourselves ... or leave our dreams behind"

Flying solo

You are on your own for the first time - it's then all up to you to fly the aircraft ...

That was it, I was now a self employed person... however with no clients and therefore no income to start with it was quite a shock from the corporate world I was used to, where the salary was paid regularly every month.

What I didn't realise at the time was the same thing that many other self employed people discover too at this point - suddenly I *had to* become my own marketing department, sales department, web designer and other roles in addition to what I really *wanted to* do - which was to help self employed people by offering them a unique service to help their businesses really take off.

With my experience gained in practice and the profession, I knew that people were worried about their tax and also about getting help, many people struggling to do it themselves thinking that they were saving money.

People regularly fail to include the value of their own time in the calculation, when they do this they find that spending a few days 'saving money' has *cost them* hundreds of pounds.

I wanted to offer them an affordable alternative, with a different experience by going to see the clients when and where was convenient to them, combined with an easy purchasing decision of an affordable fixed fee.
When I was running the tax department in practice I was helping both individuals and companies, dealing with both

personal and corporate tax. Indeed, many sole practitioners run a general practice where they help both types.

However I wanted to specialise in helping sole traders, as this was the area I enjoyed the most. Helping individuals with their new business is very rewarding. With my years of experience, I enjoy being able to simplify things for them so that they can easily understand their situation and take away the worry. Indeed, new clients are regularly commenting on how easy the process was after our first meeting.

I enjoyed helping sole trader clients but then discovered all the other work that is involved in running a business too. As I was starting from scratch, in addition I was the head of sales for my business too so I had to split my time between working and bringing in new clients.

The way that many accountants start their businesses is to buy a block of fees from a retiring accountant; however this wasn't an option both due to the availability of suitable blocks of tax fees and finances.

I'd never done any networking before then, so did the usual and joined the chamber of commerce and went to several local events on my own to see what it was about, and also tried some advertising in the local press.

In the early days, I also tried to do too much for people, rather than to do what I do now which is to specialise and refer them to other specialists where applicable, which diluted the marketing message.

This is one of the rather unusual things about business that I was to learn later. When marketing, if you say you are looking for anyone and will do anything for them - you actually end up not doing anything for anybody!

By being very specific about the clients you are looking for and what you can do for them you actually end up with *more* business, not less.

I'm not alone in that being handed a name badge and told to 'go and network' to a room full of strangers was extremely uncomfortable. I'd certainly never done anything like it before. This was like flying solo without having had any instruction.

Indeed in my early days of networking, I've seen people who either didn't turn up when they had booked a space, or who ran round handing out business cards to everyone then disappearing out the door before you had a chance to get to know more about their business ... or them.

Back then I didn't know about Ecademy or BNI so I really felt quite alone. I persisted with it though, and actually developed my own structured business agenda for networking meetings through trial and error - although it wasn't always successful as occasionally I discovered several employees at events who had been sent by their company and had a different mindset to a business owner who is looking to grow.

I also made the mistake that many people do when they start a business, and not turning away some clients. You think that you have to help everyone that approaches you, and can end up doing work that has a very low return, just because you don't want to turn it away.

After time you do learn that there are some clients that are suited to a different adviser who specialises in the area they are looking for, rather than trying to help everyone.

You also need to be prepared for time wasters as a normal part of running a business, and the small number of people any business experiences that will either cancel meetings repeatedly or just not turn up. You may want to adopt a three strikes guideline for repeated cancellations to avoid wasting time on them – plus, are they the sort of clients you would feel happy working with anyway?

In the early stages of my business one day I drove all the way to Oxford from Surrey (a return trip of over one hundred and twenty miles, in traffic) for a confirmed meeting with a new client that required several sets of accounts and tax returns completed - only to find they didn't turn up and then weren't even answering their phone. It's not much fun but it is something that I was to discover later is just a normal part of business.

Yes I was taking on new clients, but because I'd positioned myself as a unique affordable solution, I needed larger numbers rather than a few clients that might satisfy someone who was charging maybe five to ten times more than I was. So, after a few months, I was forced to take some part time subcontract roles in accountancy practices to keep the income coming in.

Having to go back to a CSC environment I didn't enjoy was not pleasant to say the least. Needs must and it just had to be done and I managed to work on my business on the days when I wasn't subcontracting, as well as the evenings and weekends. I was frustrated that I couldn't spend all my time on my own business and felt that I had taken a step backwards.

I did, however, have my first experience of serendipity at this time. I really wanted to concentrate on my own business full time and thought 'I've *got to* get some sales training to make this work.'

Whilst looking for courses to help me develop my sales skills, I discovered Tony Robbins (he's actually not a motivational or sales trainer, but that was how I'd originally found him when searching.)

Through listening to Tony Robbins audio programmes, I was able to start to understand more about myself and this knowledge translated through into my business. I was also fortunate enough to find that Tony Robbins was coming to the UK to present his 'Unleash the Power Within' seminar at the London Excel Centre.

UPW was an amazing event and quite unlike anything I'd experienced before. Along with me, there were over thirteen thousand other people there for the event, which ran over four days. It was an intense experience, Tony has a lot to say and the days were over 12 hours long, but I was surprised how quickly the time went.

At the end of the seminar, we also had the opportunity to put some of the skills we had learned into practice by fire walking, which involves storming barefoot across four metres of red hot coals which are at a temperature of around eight hundred degrees centigrade!

I have to say I was somewhat apprehensive about doing this but once I had done it, I found that it gave me a great insight. Once you have walked on fire, is there any limit to what you can achieve?

I also learned the value of contribution there and realised that *everyone* can make a difference in the world. Tony shared this, which touched me:

The Star Thrower, by Loren Eiseley:
There was a man who was walking along a sandy beach where thousands of starfish had been washed up on the shore. He noticed a boy picking the starfish one by one and throwing them back into the ocean. The man observed the boy for a few minutes and then asked what he was doing. The boy replied that he was returning the starfish to the sea, otherwise they would die.

The man asked how saving a few, when so many were doomed, would make any difference whatsoever? The boy picked up a starfish and threw it back into the ocean and said "Made a difference to that one ..."

The man left the boy and went home, deep in thought of what the boy had said. He soon returned to the beach and spent the rest of the day helping the boy throw starfish in to the sea ...

Tony also shared the fact that more than half of the world's people live below the internationally defined poverty line of less than two dollars a day. That was something I didn't know about until then.

So after the seminar in early 2008, I knew I had to make a difference and help someone. I started sponsoring a child in Honduras through one of the schemes available.

In late 2008, taxhelp.uk.com also paid to train a specialist community nurse in Honduras so that children in isolated villages showing slow growth and illness can be diagnosed, treated and cared for so they grow up fit and strong.

The shocking fact is how little it costs to make a difference in someone's life and help clear their runway for takeoff.

Tony Robbins has been a big influence and I have completed several of his audio programmes as well as returning to see him at his last London UPW seminar.

My favourite quote from Tony Robbins is:

"Quality questions create a quality life. Successful people ask better questions, and as a result, they get better answers."

Building up your hours

After your first solo, there then follows a period of time when you consolidate your experience and, after that, then you start to expand your boundaries and horizons ...

When things started to really develop for me was in June 2008, when a series of events unfolded following a 'lead generation master class' I attended, run by Richard White.

This was an interesting experience, spending a whole day thinking through what I do and what it means to my clients - putting myself in their shoes to see what they are looking to achieve and how they can be best helped.

I started to discover my USP (Unique Selling Proposition, the thing that sets you out from the competition) and indeed one of the key things that sets me apart from the typical accountant. By building my business myself from scratch, I've been through exactly the same situations as other self employed people, so I know what the challenges are and what it feels like so can connect with them on a much deeper level.

After a day spent working on the course, I was able to condense what I do into one sentence so that at once people know more about my business specifically when they ask *'what do you do?'*

"I specialise in helping self employed people in Surrey pay less tax and avoid fines."

Having this statement meant that my marketing focus could then be more specific and targeted, which then brings in better results.

It's a process I highly recommend for anyone in business, as with this established the other aspects will then flow much easier. You then know what market to target, what to pass on and your marketing can be specifically targeted towards what you are looking to achieve – rather than the 'anybody & everything' message I mentioned earlier.

It's surprising how many people I meet who can't tell me what they do exactly, in a quick and clear manner. In my early stages of networking I'd come across people who, when you asked them 'what do you do?' went on for several minutes and you still couldn't say what it was they actually did! Or some who just gave me a plain job title that didn't tell me anything about what they actually did and what made them different from anyone else with the same title.

The process I went through on the master class and its results was to come back later, and I am featured in Penny Powers book 'Know me, Like me, Follow me' because of it. This is a great example of how being more specific brings you *more* business. If you are not specific then it is difficult for people to refer you as they won't know precisely what to listen out for.

So many people at the moment try to keep all the business to themselves, rather than develop referral relationships with other businesses.

I have discovered by specialising in my own area, whilst developing relationships with other professionals who specialise in their own area we actually have *more* work passing through than if we had each solely concentrated on our own business.

Collaboration is a very powerful force, and it is one that some people are only just starting to realise the power of in the modern business world. It also means a better service for the client, and with their needs taken care of swiftly and efficiently they are then more likely to refer their friends for help too.

I also first heard about Ecademy when I was on the master class. Ecademy is a business networking community, and an amazing place where people freely share their knowledge to help others. It's a completely different environment compared to many areas of business where people may *eventually* find out what works through trial and error but then keep the knowledge to themselves as they think this will give them a business advantage over their competitors. A much healthier approach is to develop collaborative associations so that everyone wins and everyone concentrates on the specialism that they enjoy. This reminded me of how much easier it is to fly with a tail wind, rather than fighting a head wind.

Up until that point I hadn't done any online networking, so Ecademy was completely new to me. I decided to set aside half an hour a day in my diary to spend on the site and start to teach myself about it and online networking.

Online, I have found that one of the descriptions I've heard about Ecademy very much applies to all interactions on the web, something I am going to come back to many times as it is such a key concept to understanding the opportunities now available:

'A social place where business happens'

Ground crew

A pilot on their own needs a great ground crew, or network, to help and support them while they fly ...

I also joined BNI (Business Network International) in autumn 2008. BNI is an organisation that I recommend to every business owner, and is a referral organisation that helps its members to receive business through giving and receiving referrals by a structured meeting format.

BNI is now 25 years old and has developed its processes over that time. Accordingly it has a large amount of experience in what is successful in generating more business. Meetings are held weekly, as that has been proven to generate the most business for the members. BNI members in your local group carry your business card with them and actively look out for referrals for you every week.

BNI groups track the business and referrals every week, which enable them to know exactly how many thousands of pounds worth of referrals are being passed within the group. Having these statistics recorded from all the groups regularly and over time shows that each local group when it reaches its target size of forty five members will pass between three and four *million* pounds worth of business a year! I like to explain the concept to people as joining a lottery syndicate that is *guaranteed* to win every year.

Once your business begins to operate in this way, you will achieve a new level of freedom. This is much like the way the pilots of the RAF Red Arrows operate. They are individually free but working together with a high level of trust. Often they are wing tip to wing tip but have implicit faith in each others' abilities.

I remember being somewhat concerned when I heard that I would be asked to do a sixty second presentation at the meeting when I first visited - like many people who have become self employed, networking isn't something that people generally have experience of beforehand and public speaking even less so. I was nervous and about to fly solo yet again, in a different environment this time and again without instruction.

Indeed, when people are surveyed about their greatest fears death usually only comes in at number three! Public speaking and walking into a room full of strangers are feared more by most people. However, with the support available it doesn't have to be this way.

My first 'sixty seconds' was probably more like ten though, I landed with a bump as soon as it was over! The thought of doing a ten minute presentation to the group was even worse to me at that point.

However in the supportive chapter environment, and with the training courses provided by BNI, I was slowly able to develop my skills and become more comfortable doing the sixty seconds presentation.

Soon it was time for my ten minute presentation and that went ok. Afterwards I was surprised how quickly the time seemed to go.

After four months, I was offered the role of Secretary Treasurer - they must have seen the accountant in me coming! I took the role with both hands as it meant being part of the leadership team and having to make a short presentation at the front of the room to the chapter and visitors weekly.

Three months later I was asked if I would like to be Chapter Director. I really wasn't sure about this as I would be running the meetings each week and it would be quite a bit outside my comfort zone, however it was a supportive environment and I would receive training in how to do it, so I accepted. Now I would be running the ninety minute meetings each week, when a few months before I could barely manage ten seconds! I'd gone from nervous flyer to squadron leader, what was I thinking?

This went well and over my leadership term I was able to develop until I was fairly comfortable about presenting to a group of people.

Dr Misner talked recently about the butterfly effect and how one event can lead to others; this is certainly something I've experienced thanks to my membership of BNI and my development there.

Since my term as Chapter Director, I have presented to several different networking groups about my own business and also about social networking of which I am a prolific advocate. On the back of being featured in Penny Powers' book, I was offered a chance to present to fifty financial advisers in London and, armed with my BNI presenting experience, I accepted.

After my term as chapter director finished, I was also offered the chance to become an assistant director for BNI. This involves looking after chapters, presenting to them and running training courses for members.

This was the next level and would give me a chance to learn more so I accepted. I attended director training then shortly afterwards went to the US International Directors' Conference in Long Beach, California.

I learnt a lot there with other directors freely sharing their knowledge and as well as meeting Dr Ivan Misner in person. I also first heard about the BNI author mentee program there, which provides assistance to BNI members so that they can develop their writing skills. I've been using the help for blogging and thanks to the support received this book has been possible.

The butterfly effect continues to come into play, recently I was offered the chance to test fly a new twin engine aircraft and write up my experiences, so the skills I've developed meant this was an easy task and I had the review completed the same day I flew the aircraft. I did at least wait until I landed to write it up though! The review is to be published in Flyer magazine, one of the UK's leading aviation magazines.

As an assistant director for BNI, I am now looking after two chapters myself and helping the members to develop and the chapters to grow and generate more business. As well as that, I am also a BNI member myself and am the current Secretary/Treasurer in the recently launched Esher & Cobham chapter.

The Esher & Cobham chapter is special as it holds the current record for the largest ever BNI visitors' day in Surrey. Thanks to all our hard work we had one hundred and thirty eight guests attend, in addition to our own twenty chapter members.

As an Assistant Director, I was also very pleased to find that one of my chapters I look after, BNI Kingswood, was ranked the number one chapter in Surrey in August 2010 - and was also ranked fifteenth out of all the UK BNI chapters. They have worked hard and grown the chapter from nineteen members just over six months ago to its current level of over forty.

When I started with BNI, giving a sixty second presentation to a few people was extremely uncomfortable. Now I regularly present to audiences of between thirty and forty people and have presented at team leader training to audiences of over one hundred people.

I also run trainings for BNI in Spain regularly as well. Having the same proven structure worldwide means that this is quite straightforward, and the two chapters I visit on the South coast of Spain also hold their meetings in English.

I'm very grateful for BNI and how I have developed personally, going back two years there was no way I would have believed I'd be standing in front of audiences of over one hundred people and training them.

Gail Nott said recently on Twitter that her BNI theme for the next year is to 'learn more to earn more'. This is something I very much agree with. With the training and support available through BNI, this knowledge is freely available and is one of the benefits of membership.

There are many courses available to BNI members that are not just about getting the most out of BNI, they also have great value on their own for the general business knowledge they pass on. These would cost hundreds of pounds for someone to attend normally, but through BNI often they cost not much more than a normal breakfast meeting fee.

Outside of my business private flying is still my passion, and I wouldn't be able to afford my own aeroplane without the successful growth in my company that has come through being a BNI member.

As well as my own personal growth through BNI, my business has grown significantly since I joined and that's during a recession (that we as BNI members refuse to participate in.)

Givers Gain® is the key to my success and BNI's strapline. The principle is simple and it works. I help members with the training so that they can generate more business and also use the same techniques myself to generate referrals for my fellow chapter members. In return they pass me business and help my company grow. It's almost like having your plane refuelled for free in mid-air. Now there's a thought!

Joining BNI was definitely the best business decision I've ever made.

The glass cockpit

In classic aircraft the instruments were simple dials, now these are being replaced with modern flat panel glass cockpits. This development carries through to the changes that are happening in the business world now ...

Shortly after joining BNI, I heard Penny Power, the founder of Ecademy, speak at the BNI South East members' day, which really inspired me about the possibilities of combining offline and online networking.

People may think that online networking is solely online, but through the connections I have made online I have learnt a huge amount about social networking and have also regularly attended the local Ecademy offline events. For example, the Guildford event was where I first met Nick Tadd and Vanessa Warwick.

I also met Tom Evans at the Weybridge Ecademy club - he talked there about writing, and I picked up tips that helped me writing my blogs and also to publish this story. Before then I hadn't posted much publicly as I'd never had the experience of doing this, and was worried about what people would think about my postings. Like most people when they start blogging, it wasn't something I was comfortable with.

Since then I have combined online and offline networking with great results and have discovered that with both of these you don't necessarily get an instant result - it takes time to build up a reputation and for people to know, like and trust you.

I can apply principles I have learnt in one environment to the other, with equally good results.

This is a bit like flying. Although you might think all the fun is when you are in the air, carrying out important work on the ground makes the flight much more rewarding. By looking at the weather conditions, you can fly with a tail wind, avoid turbulence and storms and, of course, ensure that your destination airport is actually open!

I have also met many good friends through Ecademy and BNI, and the things I have learned mean that I can now use these skills to help other people in the situation I was in a few years ago. I have given several talks to local networking groups and businesses on 'Social Networking for business' and how it has really changed things for me.

What I'd like to share with people that are self employed is how much help is available to you, particularly through Ecademy and BNI.

After being an Ecademy member for a couple of years, I joined their BlackStar membership. This is a level that facilitates greater interaction between serious networkers - as well as providing tools on the website to save time and promote your services.

As part of the membership I had my first experience of the 'BlackStar Boardroom'. Many self employed people do not have a board of directors or indeed many people that they can sound out ideas with. What the boardroom does is provide this, through groups of around 12 people that meet monthly.

It's bit like having 12 navigators to help you with your flight plan.

This resource is incredibly valuable as the *navigators* attending each boardroom meeting usually change, and each person brings a different perspective, and map, depending on their own business experience. The meetings follow a structured format to gain the most out of them, and are strictly confidential under 'the Chatham House rule' so that people can freely discuss any issues they may have, whether business or personal.

Under the Chatham House Rule, participants are free to use the information received, but neither the identity nor the affiliation of the speaker(s), nor that of any other participant, may be revealed.

So, from joining Ecademy initially as an online network, I was actually now regularly attending offline meetings too, which were having a positive effect on my business.

Many people at the moment dismiss online networking, not realising that it can actually lead to offline networking and meetings – the real power of online networking is that it enables you to connect quickly and without travel time, wherever you may be.

It also enables you to connect with and keep in touch with people after the offline meeting. I am regularly in contact with several of my BNI chapter members through twitter and Facebook outside of our weekly face to face meetings.

Online networking can also *bring* you business, without you having to go and look for it.

I was in a networking meeting a while ago run by Nick Tadd and Vanessa Warwick where Vanessa was putting messages on Twitter telling the web what was happening in the meeting. We went round the room doing quick introductions and one of the people there ran a business cleaning carpets. The power of the interaction available online was shown when someone messaged Vanessa and asked for a quote from the carpet cleaner! They weren't in the room, but were able to take part in our networking event thanks to social networking. The carpet man's business was magically flying that evening!

I very much agree that the power in online networking is that you combine it with offline networking too.

As for normal face to face netWORKing, the WORK part of social networking is important too, you need to have a goal of what you are looking to achieve online; otherwise the time can be wasted. The ultimate aim is to carry it out so you are NOTworking all the time.

Thomas Power estimates that it can take one to three years of being online before you see the real benefits, and this is something I would definitely agree with. It was well over eighteen months since I started networking online before I was seeing the first results. After two and a half years, these results are now significant.

Many people 'try' social networking for a few months and then give up ... that's a bit like getting to the end of the runway and switching off your engine.

If you stick with it, you could find that, as with offline networking, results really start to come in from the end of the first year onwards.

Crossing the ocean

After a period of flying locally, many pilots seek out further adventures ...

How big is your network? Is it your local town? Maybe it's your county? Or, could it even be as big as the whole country?

How about the world?

I discovered that it is surprisingly easy to be known internationally now as well.

As I am a director for BNI in Surrey, when I was in Spain for a few days I was offered the opportunity to present a training seminar to local BNI chapters - which was then promoted by the head of BNI in Spain.

So, from my Surrey BNI role I was now presenting internationally - and as BNI uses the same format world wide it is easy to visit meetings in other countries and feel comfortable.

As well as the BNI connection, I also met a fellow Ecademy member at the meeting Keith Spitalnick and as a result we are connected through Twitter and communicating on Ecademy as well now - showing how the online and offline worlds combine.

You may think that your networking is just local, but by using the same procedures here in the UK, I found it is very easy to expand this internationally.

Similarly this change affects your business online too. A comment I hear regularly is people complaining that someone in another country wants to connect with them online. They think that this is a waste of time as they don't want to connect with someone there, as there is no possibility of them working together.

That may be, but what about the other person's connections? They may have family or friends in your country that could very much be potential customers, but if you don't make the connection you could be missing out on the business. I've heard it said 'it's not who you know, it's who *they know* that's important' – something that many people don't always appreciate.

When I started online networking, I was contacted by a lady in Canada through Ecademy and we started messaging online about our businesses. As it turned out, after we had leant more about each other's businesses, she had family in the UK who could be potential clients. If I hadn't accepted that initial contact we wouldn't have discovered this.

Being open, random and supportive as advocated by Penny and Thomas Power is the key to success online.

My videos and website, as well as all my social networking content, is available to a worldwide audience and not just locally.

There are many changes happening now in the business world and the great thing is that you don't have to go through the process of trial and error yourself. There are many people worldwide, like myself, who have been through this and are happy to share their experiences so you don't have to waste time learning what *doesn't* work.

There are whole communities out there that can support you - you only have to ask.

When you are up in the air, you don't have to be very high to see that the Earth is curved. If you stay grounded, your horizons will always be limited.

I have achieved more in six months through the combination of social networking and BNI than in the whole first two years of self employment struggling to find things out myself.

Unable to comply

This is a phrase pilots say when they can't complete the standard procedures that everyone else is following ...

Similarly, 'refusing to participate in a recession' is something I picked up through BNI, and is a statement I have proved myself during the most recent financial meltdown.

Usually for accountants, January is the busiest month of the year, followed by February and March being very quiet. This is considered 'normal' and many people in the industry just accept it as being part of the annual business cycle.

In 2010, I had our company's *busiest week ever* for new clients, in February! This is why and how.

Many people just accept market conditions as normal and unfortunately they can then become an excuse for people to not just try harder. For example: 'it's ok, it's normally quiet in the summer in our industry', 'our sales are down due to the recession', etc.

The new clients we have taken on, in what was considered a traditionally quiet month of the year, were a mixture of people that included those who had missed the tax return deadline, some who were several years behind, and those who are either looking to start a self employed business or change their existing accountant before the new tax year.

I thought that it could be useful to share how we have achieved this, when most of the competition was sitting around just accepting that it's a quiet time of year, as it may also be of benefit in your own business to bring in more clients:

1)   Be a person, not a business name
So many people's websites don't even say their own name and just have the trading name - people want to know who it is they are dealing with, and some details about who they are as a person.

This is why I shot a series of videos with Nick Tadd and Vanessa Warwick last year and have put these on many pages of our website so that people can see who I am in the video interview, as well as sharing personal information about myself. When you get on any commercial flight, the pilot always tells you over the intercom who you are flying with. When you are in an unnatural environment 5 miles above the Earth, it's nice to know whose hands your life is in.

On this note, our biggest client last year actually contacted me after reading my Ecademy profile - what attracting him was my flying adventures, rather than what you would have thought - my two decades of business experience and my qualifications in tax and accounts. We actually spent over an hour at the first meeting discussing flying.

2)   Be flexible in meeting times
Clients have their own business to run so taking time away from this to see you can have a detrimental effect, and can cost them a significant amount in lost working time. I am flexible as to when I will see people to fit in with their schedule. It's not just the cost of *your service*; it's the cost of *their time* in using you that you need to account for as well.

In February, I saw people at times ranging from 11am on a Sunday to 9pm on a Thursday.

As a BNI director, I'm even up early many mornings and also happy to meet people before 6:30am when they visit meetings as well. Being up at that time of day means that any travelling time is massively reduced and usually people actually find themselves arriving too early as they are only used to travelling during the normal business hours.

3)   Be flexible as to meeting locations

Many businesses require the client to come to see them in their office. With commuting time this can mean a client could potentially lose half a day's work.

I will visit clients wherever is most convenient for them - whether it is local to where they are working at lunchtime, at their home in the evening or wherever is easiest. Clients really appreciate it when you fit in with their needs.

Yes, there is a cost to my business of doing this, but it is important to meet the client and establish the relationship – face to face is the best way to do this and it's an investment I consider to be essential.

Once you have met face to face, all other correspondence may be by email or telephone, but you have made that initial connection so have more of an understanding.

4)   Network extensively

I network extensively, both online and offline - this is important as it can take over a year to build relationships with people before they may do business with you.

Many people expect to get an instant result from networking, whereas if you are consistent then the results will come *in time*.

You need to allocate the time and stick with it. BNI has a great saying describing the process of developing relationships, 'farming, rather than hunting', and you need to plant the seeds of success and spend enough time cultivating them.

5)   Don't always use traditional marketing methods

My marketing plan in early 2009 was to use an extensive flyer campaign, which wasted several thousand pounds and which I won't be repeating.

Vanessa Warwick's article is something I will mention later and it is something which I regularly refer to as it is important to realise that expensive traditional methods may not be relevant to your own business. Don't listen to the new self-proclaimed gurus who don't use their own methods.

For a small business trying to use traditional marketing methods, you are competing with others who may have much larger budgets, so it can be difficult to gain an effective result.

The power of the digital economy is that everyone now has the same potential influence available to them, and the budget available isn't the deciding factor.

6)   Be easily contactable

So many websites, as well as not telling you the person's name, don't even have their phone number or email address!

I have openly published my email address and phone number for the last few years online and don't suffer from mountains of spam. If you make it difficult for people to contact you they may just give up and go to a competitor.

Our website has an extensive 'contact us' section which lists all the places people can connect with me, and I've also listed these later in the resources chapter. I regularly use my custom signature block in online postings and blogs. This was created by Ces Loftus and makes it easy to see how to contact me without having to waste time looking.

I've had new clients from Twitter, Facebook and Ecademy to name a few - different ages of clients prefer different methods of contacting you.

I regularly communicate via Twitter and text message, depending on the client, whereas some clients prefer the telephone and others email. Skype is something I use regularly too, particularly when calling long distance and internationally.

At this point I'd also like to share a couple of tips regarding web and email addresses that many people don't consider:

1) Make sure you have your own domain and email address. People starting in business don't realise affects how people perceive their quality.

   Clients are more likely to want to connect with someone who has 'joe@yourprofession.com' as their email address rather than 'joe234587@hotmail.com' – the cost of this is very affordable and it is easy to set up.

I have even seen vans with huge sign writing on the side which has a Hotmail address, so it's not uncommon for people to make this mistake.

2) For your domain name you want something memorable, but it also has to be fairly short as potential clients will be contacting you through it, both on email and through your website – they will be typing it in, so are they likely to do this or give up and use a competitor?

   'www.joesprofessionalswereallyaregreat.com' may sound great but it's not a good idea. I have seen it done many times though. There is also the option of having several sites, and maybe redirecting people from a short address to the longer one if you really want to do this.

Different clients will have their own preferred method of contacting you, whether by phone, email, text, etc ...

Incidentally, The Bookwright, Tom Evans, is a master of how to maximise your impact with just a few words and runs workshops on the subject of "You Only Have 1 Second". He is also brilliant at coming up with snappy book titles (like mine) and domain names.

Make yourself contactable on all platforms so that it as easy as possible for people to get hold of you

Aviate, navigate, communicate

When flying a plane this is the order of priorities to follow to ensure a successful outcome, and it very much applies to business too – do the technical work, know where you are going and then tell people about it ...

People used to talk about 'surfing the web', which can be described as web 1.0 – where people looked for information online and then *downloaded* it or *viewed* it. The web was just taxiing at this time.

Now we are in Web 2.0 – where people now create content then *upload it* to share. This is where the web really has started to take off.

One thing I do fairly often is to blog about my experiences, and also write articles for various websites and magazines.

There are many benefits to writing, both in increased visibility as well as starting conversations that can lead to beneficial discussions and maybe result in business as well.

Blogs should be used for sharing knowledge and experiences, rather than as an out and out sales tool. This is a trap some people fall into.

I blog on a variety of subjects, both business and personal, interestingly the personal blogs quite often lead to business anyway!

People want to do business with other people, so sharing your personal interests lets people know more about you and they are then more likely to want to do business with you as a person, rather than just as a company.

This can be a difficult concept to understand when you are coming from the corporate world. In the corporate world your identity in most cases is the company you represent, not you as an individual.

As a sole trader you and the business are very much linked, and the same entity.

An example of this can be seen by a couple of blogs I wrote in March and April 2010.

My first blog talked about the issues with communicating internationally and the opportunities it represented for business owners worldwide, titled 'A quick and easy way to boost a business.'

My second blog was a personal one about a long weekend at Portmeirion that came about due to my being a Mensa member, titled 'Portmeirion – what's that?'

Both of these blogs are reprinted in the navigator's guide.

So, what was the result of these two blogs?

At the time of writing, my personal blog had a *third more* views and over *two and a half times more* comments!

This proves the point that it's not always just about talking about the business side that generates interest.

As a result of sharing the personal side, I have had many new clients who first heard of me and became interested in my services through some personal information I have shared.

Indeed, as I've mentioned, my biggest client so far came through Ecademy, and the thing that interested him initially was me sharing about my interest in flying - not my years of experience and specialism in personal tax, which you would have thought would have been what he was looking for. When we met we spent a considerable amount of time chatting about flying after we had done the business, as this was one of his interests too.

I regularly get people who have heard of my flying adventures, and because this interests them and starts a conversation, they then use my services.

What is the cost of blogging?
It's nothing, apart from your own time, and it gets much easier the more you do it. When I first started it was hard work for me to do a short blog, whereas recently I had a website ask me for a one thousand word article and it was very easy to do this quickly from my experience.

You don't even need to spend time in front of a computer sitting at a desk writing either. In the past many of my blogs were written on a Netbook computer I used to use. Now the iPad has replaced this and it is even easier.

Sometimes on holiday or when travelling on business, I may have a blog idea and with my iPad I can open up the word processor and start writing wherever I am and then even post it online too. Researching topics and adding links to content is easy too. Indeed, sections of this book were written and edited on my iPad while I was travelling.
I also regularly use my iPhone to contribute to blogs. As well as this it is easy to shoot high definition video and

photographs on it and from there edit and upload them to the web. These can then form additions to my blogs, and the great benefit that all this is done remotely, wherever I am, without having to wait until I am back in the office.

Again, sharing a video I shot while flying brought me a new client who saw this initially and it then led them through to my website and finding out more about my business.

Audio recordings also make a great blog and most mobile phones can now record audio so you don't need expensive equipment to capture your thoughts. There are even artists who use pen and paper and photograph their art and then post it online.

Age is not a factor either. At the time of writing, the world's oldest blogger, Maria Amelia Lopez, passed away last year at 97 and the world's oldest Twitterer, Ivy Bean, was 104 before she unfortunately died.

An important lesson I learnt from Tom Evans that has really helped me:

When you have an idea, for a blog, an article, or a story you must write it down - capture it right then, otherwise it will be lost and you may find someone else getting great results from an idea you had first, but failed to act upon

Hidden in the clouds?

On a radar screen full of many blips, how do you identify one specific aircraft from the others? 'Squawking ident' highlights you on the screen so you can be found easily ...

I have now become known as 'the Twittering tax man' - a few years ago I hadn't even used social networking, so it's very much a skill that anyone can pick up.

The moniker of the Twittering tax man developed from my involvement online, people knew me from social networking and also my involvement in tax. I was meeting with Richard White, the master of the archetype, one day at his training centre, and when I walked in he looked up and said 'it's the Twittering tax man' – I thought that was perfect and adopted it.

In everyone's business there is something about them and what they do that is different. By focussing on this you can find that you have actually created a brand as a natural part of your growth.

These are our call signs and, as for aircraft, what people use to identify us by and with. People will be attracted by them or perhaps know that it's not of interest and avoid us. Either way, it ensures the right type of traffic is directed our way.

Outside of my core business, I have also given my time to run presentations to people on social networking and how it has helped my business. With my experiences online people look to me for advice on how to get started and I am happy to share this, as I was in their situation myself only a few years ago.

Indeed I remember being booked to present at a local networking event, held in a large serviced office nearby, to talk about my experiences with social networking.

The handout just had my name and company name, so when I started talking about social networking it grabbed the attention of some audience members who had just been expecting a standard talk about tax returns!

As with the comments I made earlier on blogging, where sharing personal information brings you business, I have found that sharing my knowledge on social networking also brings me business too.

Business starts with a conversation and I have found whether this is on social topics or social media, once you are conversing business will likely flow naturally. You don't have to always be pushing your business in order to generate business.

Dr Misner recently blogged about brands and how they mean so much more to people than a logo and it's something I found myself recently when I considered changing my brand.

He shared a definition that he came across from Tilka Design about how a brand lives in the imagination:

"Intuitively, we all know what a brand is. It's far more than a logo. And it's much larger than a product, service, idea or institution. A brand finds its home in the minds and hearts of individuals; it's made up of stories and experiences that, over time, create feelings. When enough people share those feelings, the brand comes to life."

Through a blog I asked for feedback from my Ecademy connections and found huge support amongst the people I'd met to retain 'the Twittering tax man.'

As well as Penny Power's response to my blog, 'It tells everyone that you are on Social Media and up to date, and they know where to find you.' There were also great feelings expressed by people who had developed relationships with me over time, as well as from people who hadn't actually met me, but had been following me online.

I meet people at networking events sometimes, who I've never met before, and they come up to me and say 'you're the Twittering tax man' - this is all through social media and sharing my information, I haven't spent many thousands of pounds on a Twittering tax man brand awareness campaign, that may have been the traditional way to do this in the past.

In developing a brand online I have found the process is very much as described by Penny Power:

"Know me, like me, follow me"

Once people get to know what you are about and they like it, they will follow your homing beacon naturally

You have control

*Being pilot in command of a light aircraft means that you have the freedom to choose **your** destination, and can also share airspace with much larger aircraft **on an equal footing** ...*

Here is one of the great changes in the business world today:

YOU now have the same influence as any large corporation!

An example of this is the power of brands and how it is now available to everyone at low cost.

I was at an Ecademy networking event a while ago, where Vanessa Warwick was talking about how things have now shifted from the vertical to the horizontal, an image which I found to be very inspirational:

The ladder has fallen
In the past the closed, restrictive & controlling society meant that there was a vertical ladder - with individuals at the bottom and large corporations at the top.

The old ways meant that the more you spent on marketing, the more your message was heard. The costs involved prevented individuals and small businesses from competing at the same level. Vanessa talked about how this is no longer the case, and we are now seeing a return to the individual.
With the spread of the web and social media, now one individual can have the same *or greater* influence, regardless of the amount spent.

The vertical has moved to the horizontal

Just consider this:

Ashton Kutcher has many more followers on Twitter than CNN yet how much do CNN spend on marketing?

The Susan Boyle YouTube video. How much would a company have had to spend on marketing to get their video viewed ten million times?

I recently tweeted a link to a Wall Street Journal article on the spread of laptop use amongst the homeless. Now that technology prices have fallen so low for second-hand computers and with old ones even being given away, combined with the availability of free wireless access - everyone has the same potential influence.

When I mentioned this, Vanessa commented:

"It must be recognised that we are now living in exponential times as we are now in the era of the networked or linked economy and this is an environment where the individual can thrive. A small effort is amplified through networks, meaning that you can benefit from the law of increasing returns."

Business is becoming up close and personal again, and this favours the small business or individual as we can offer a much more personal interface with the customer than a corporation can.

A single-engine aircraft is like an SME. They are much more nimble than corporations who are more like a jumbo jet. Corporate business need long runways to take off and land from. They can't economically fly without a full load of passengers. We can take off and land just when we want and where we want on so many more airfields.

As most of the social media and social networking tools and sites are FREE, this means that there is an almost non-existent barrier to entry in social media engagement. What you do need is some technical skills to create web content, a strong opinion on your niche area of expertise, and some writing talent to ensure that your output shines out through the on-line "noise".

Social media engagement and participation allows the man on the street to reach the same global audience as a corporation.

An example is the author Anna Sam. A year ago, Anna worked as a checkout assistant in a supermarket in Rennes in France. She started writing a blog about her experiences of working on a checkout. Her blog built up a following of readers who enjoyed her unique writing style. The blog eventually came to the attention of a publisher who offered her a publishing deal. She has now sold over 100,000 copies of her book and is in negotiation for the film rights. So, she self-published her material on the web, which cost her nothing, and it has led to this! Her talent was given a platform to shine through and reach a global market place. This would have been impossible even five years ago.

Closer to my home, someone I know personally, Sally Asling of Surrey Lets, is a good example of a one woman band working from home that is enjoying the same business exposure as a major high street letting agent. Sally generated over six thousand pounds worth of business from Twitter in three months.

Thomas and Penny Power are leading thinkers in this evolving world of social media and one of the great benefits of being a member of Ecademy is that we can learn from them and benefit by being early adopters of this new way of spreading our messages on-line. We are probably eighteen months away from mass participation, so those of us who build our on-line profile and reputation now will benefit hugely when this hits the mainstream.

Nick Tadd also believe that social media engagement and participation is the only way to future-proof your business. Nick has even become a bit of a social media rock star and is really entertaining to listen to and follow on Twitter. He trades constantly in what has become known as the Twittersphere.

Indeed, I was able to demonstrate this when a lady sent a message out on Twitter a while ago asking for urgent help with a quick tax/accounts query.

I was the only person to reply to this in the whole of the UK!

No-one from any of the big accountancy firms, or anyone else from the thousands of small and medium accountancy practices throughout the UK replied.

With the case of the big firms, they have marketing budgets that can run into millions of pounds - yet hardly any have embraced the use of Social Networking, which is low cost and can be very effective.

We have taken on several new clients through Twitter, as well as the increased visibility and the opportunities that have arisen due to my contributions made there. All at no cost, apart from a little time.

For the larger firms, it wouldn't actually cost them much to have a young tax senior on the staff, whose full time job was to monitor Twitter and other social networking sites for their whole UK office network and to reply or refer when needed.

In fact, as far as I am aware, I am one of very few people in the UK who has really embraced Twitter and social networking from my profession (Mark Lee is another - @bookMarkLee) - it's also the reason I have become 'the Twittering tax man' without any competition.

With the low costs associated with social networking, and the benefits available, I would definitely recommend that people get on board **now** to get an advantage over their competitors (which could even be the very top firms in the country, as I found.)

An excellent quote I heard recently, when it comes to the changes in business now happening:

You are either on the train or you are under it

In-Flight entertainment

Checks complete, we have filed a flight plan and are ready for departure. We need to keep our passengers fed, watered and occupied en route ...

Would you like a business advantage? Imagine if you could not only educate your client but entertain them at the same time. I've heard this called edutainment and it's becoming one of the best and quickest ways to grab clients' attention.

I would like to share an example of a client we took on and how the process differed from the traditional way of doing things, which shows how video and short real-time interactions can make a difference.

As I've mentioned, I decided to get some videos for my website to explain the various pages in detail and to let people 'meet me' beforehand. The advantage of these is that they are available 24/7 for people to look at whenever it's convenient *for them*. It also helps people get to know me better and what I do when they can actually see me speaking.

Having videos on many of our individual web pages means that it also saves time in the initial contact and meeting - if they have already watched you talking about the service, you don't need to cover this again and they can then ask any questions they may have in more depth.

The client taken on had watched my videos and then contacted me via the message box on our website to make an initial enquiry - this came through on Sunday morning to my BlackBerry. We had a few short messages back and forth to arrange a meeting in Cobham for the following week. As he had seen the videos he already knew the details of our services.

This was all arranged while other peoples' offices were closed, and it only took a few minutes overall.

With the change in lifestyle, the traditional nine to five time slot isn't always convenient for clients to contact you. By making it as easy as possible for people to find out about you and then get in touch, using whichever method is best for them, is a great way to differentiate your service.

The secret about video

I discovered a while ago that YouTube was actually ranked as the second highest search engine and thought that this could have possibilities for helping people to hear about me and maybe start to understand what I do.

This surprised me - I Googled 'accountant surrey' and there were over half a million websites whereas if you choose the 'video' tab there were only about twenty results!

Video is another great opportunity to get ahead.

It is so easy to do this. I now have my own free YouTube channel, and when Nick Tadd sent me the video files we shot I uploaded them myself.

I also have a blip.tv channel which can also create an audio file of my videos and it also link into iTunes for video podcasts. People can then download my videos as a video podcast and watch them on their iPod, iPhone or iPad wherever it is convenient to them. It was very easy to do all of this; I'd never used any of these sites before but picked up the basics quickly.

So from one easy video session I now have an increased web presence, as well as being able to link to the videos to use on my website, on blogs and my online profiles as well as in emails, etc.

As well as videos giving people more information at a time and place when it is convenient *for them*, one other advantage is that some people like to start them playing and then also read the key points of text of a website or blog while they listen to the audio track from your video.

It also shows the importance of having a quality video recorded - many videos are just people talking straight to a camera, usually a basic webcam, and with a messy filing cabinet behind them.

Compare this to the high definition interview style of my own videos, which were shot outside on a sunny day.

It is also very affordable to have a professional video recorded - the ones I shot had, within a couple of weeks, already paid for themselves through a new client taken on. They will continue to bring in new clients over the coming months - as well as being great tools for people to get to know me better before we meet.

With the increase in use of location based services, such as Foursquare and Gowalla, we are now seeing *another opportunity* for people to connect with you in real time.

Rather than connecting with a client at a later date there is the opportunity to connect with them while they are still nearby and I've included a section on this in the navigator's guide.

I will end this chapter with a salutary thought from Nick Tadd:

The return on investment from social media is that you will actually still have a business in a few years time!

Cleared for takeoff

Now it's time to leave the ground behind and take to the sky ...

Vanessa Warwick also posted a blog in April 2009, in her property forum, which I feel should be shared with everyone in business as the comments are equally valid.

It so neatly encapsulates what I wanted to share in this chapter that it is included here in entirety with her permission.

Her blog explained the changes in business that are occurring and how the old ways of marketing are disappearing, something that I had found to my cost with my own initial campaigns, before reading her article.

By adopting the philosophy in this blog, you will be flying solo in no time at all.

Her blog had an attention grabbing headline:

**'Still leafleting .... placing ads in the newspaper?
YOU ARE WASTING YOUR TIME AND MONEY!
Wake up and smell the social media ...'**

If you are still leafleting, placing ads in your local newspaper etc. you are wasting your time and your money. Almost everything is on-line now, or will be within the next few years, so why use marketing platforms that are contracting and shrinking on a daily basis? Shouldn't you be embracing these new ways of spreading your messages? If you did, might it put you ahead of the competition and give you a flying head start when the property market turns around?

With the advent of Web 2.0, the consumer realises that they have a choice in what marketing messages they are exposed to.

Leaflets through the door
Are treated as spam and unfortunately in many cases go straight in the bin. Research has proven this to be the case time and time again. It takes hours to leaflet even a few streets, when, by going on line I can expose my marketing message to thousands of people interested in what I have to say if I know where they can be found on line.

Newspaper ads
People go on-line to find their accommodation now. Think about it. Most people under forty (your prospective tenants) were brought up in the digital age, so it is natural for them to go on-line to look for stuff. They won't be reading your newspaper advert, which has cost you money to place. They will be looking on sites where you can advertise for free!

Some facts for your consideration:

1)   People now communicate more regularly via social networks than they do by email.

2)   Social networking is not just for teenagers. In 2008, 35 - 49 year olds represented the biggest growth segment for the social networking sector. Some people are choosing to ignore Social Media as they think it is "just for kids". It isn't. Don't make the same mistake in your business. People spend more time in social networks when they're online.

3)   Nielsen Research noted that, here in the UK, one in every six minutes online, was being spent in, or on, the social networking websites making them stand out clearly as the places where more and more people are choosing to connect.

4)   Despite the recession, most marketers are increasing their spend on Social Media.

If you know where your target audience is located on line, then you can connect with them.

For example, you should log onto forums that talk about what your potential clients are talking about. Engage in conversations with people and offer than advice. Then, if they get to the stage where they may need your services, they will trust you, as you tried to help them.

This is called "contribution currency" and it's all about building trust in on-line networks.

Everything starts with a conversation. Social media are the tools you use to start dialogues on-line.

So, if you are thinking of wasting your money on another newspaper ad, did you know that twenty two percent of internet users have ditched their newspapers?

In many cases, yes, according to a recent study by the University of Southern California's Annenberg School for Communication. It found that twenty two percent of Internet users have cancelled a print subscription because they could get the same product online.

Not that nostalgia for the printed page has died altogether. The survey found that sixty one percent of internet users who read newspapers offline would miss the print edition if it disappeared. That's up from fifty six percent a year earlier.

The findings add some dimension to industry figures released this week showing newspapers losing circulation faster than ever. Average newspaper sales tumbled over seven percent in the six months from October to March from the same period a year earlier, according to an Audit Bureau of Circulations analysis of newspapers that had reported in both periods.

Some of that decline, as newspapers are quick to point out, comes from cutting back on what they consider less-profitable circulation - bulk copies delivered to hotels, for instance. But the Annenberg study suggests a more rapid and permanent shift, according to its authors.

Jeffrey Cole, head of the Annenberg School's Centre for a Digital Future, recalled his prediction nearly ten years ago that print newspapers would soldier on for another twenty or twenty five years.

"We always thought it was a generational thing," he said. "It turned out I was an optimist." Cole says the flight of advertisers from daily newspapers - a trend exacerbated by the recession - is likely to usher printed news into the past over the next few years.

Already this year some newspapers have shut down, eliminated publication days or cut delivery to a few days a week.

Cole said one thing is certain for anyone over thirty: "When the printed newspaper goes away, breakfast just won't make sense."

The random survey of 2,030 people ages twelve and up was conducted April 9 to June 30, 2008, and has a margin of sampling error of plus or minus three percentage points.

Our very own Sally of Surrey Lets is successfully using Twitter to find tenants. Twitter is FREE! I advertise our holiday lets via Twitter and other social and business networking sites. These are FREE to use and I am reaching a global marketplace. Because people have subscribed to my Twitter stream they have chosen to be exposed to my messages! So I have a receptive audience, who trust me, and are interested in what I tweet! THAT is the future of business. Not spam that has no value and is a one way channel.

Social media is a two way channel that allows you to interact with your followers and find out what they need and want.

So are you going to be carrying on with dying ways of marketing or are you going to wake up and smell the social media?

So many people are trying things because 'everyone else does it' thinking that that's just what you do when you start a business. People who do this don't share the fact that things have changed and it's not working much anymore because of their CSC nature – they think it must be their problem and that everyone else is doing ok, because no one is sharing the fact that things have changed.

As I mentioned, I spent many thousands of pounds and hours on a marketing campaign using flyers that, if I had read Vanessa's blog first, I wouldn't have done.

However, there is no such thing as a failure provided you learn from the experience.

At the time I thought that this would be a good way to grow the business. In past years marketing in this way was a fairly easy and reliable way to grow a business - you send out one thousand flyers and had maybe a one to two percent response rate, from which you would maybe convert a total of half a percent from the initial one thousand flyers into new clients. For years these rates were fairly static and you knew if you wanted more clients all you had to do was sent out more flyers - a simple numbers game.

Except, with the rise of the web, this method doesn't work anymore - people's attention is being demanded in so many different locations that they are starting to 'tune out' to many of them. I found that my flyers were generating a hundred times less than the expected response rate, so whilst they were generating some new business the cost per new client taken on was unaffordable as it would take many years to recoup the initial marketing spend at my particular pricing level.

Traditional newspaper advertising was also something I'd tried, again with limited success. Yes, it was bringing in a few new clients but the costs per client were too high.

Frank Kern said:
'Be grateful if your traditional marketing methods are failing now - in the future they will fail for everyone and it gives you an advantage to get ahead.'

With the help I have received both on and offline I have been consistently growing the client base over the last few years, and been able to help more people ranging from new start ups (some of whom have been made redundant themselves) to existing businesses looking to reduce their outgoings.

For me, I have found that the secret to success with online and offline networking is the BNI motto 'Givers Gain'® combined with an Open Random & Supportive (ORS) attitude.

For example, whenever possible now, when I see someone who is 'lost' at a networking event I apply a BNI technique which is to pretend to be the host of the event and start up a conversation and introduce them to people I know. I'd been 'lost' at networking events when I started so I know exactly how it felt. Dr Misner talks about this and other simple techniques in more detail in his book 'Networking Like a Pro.'

This technique can also be applied online by helping new users to learn about the systems when they are just starting.

As I mentioned, I was the only adviser in the entire UK to reply to a plea for help on Twitter, which shows an example of how this giving attitude can actually mean that you are the leader in your field - and you don't require a massive marketing budget to do it.

Now that you have the secret, how do you make it work?

Keep going

So many people are so close to success and they stop just before they reach it. It's something I've sadly seen many times both online and offline. This is just like doing a circuit from an airfield where you never get higher than

1000 feet and you just land back exactly where you started. Great fun but hardly satisfying.

Comparing the adventure I've been on over the last few years to how things could have been if I hadn't been made redundant, and had still been an employee, I realise that I wouldn't have reached anything like my potential.

The changes in business and the emergence of the digital economy will happen to everyone, if you embrace them now you can have an advantage over your competitors that can't be beaten.

I'd like to leave you with a quote from Tony Robbins that kept me going when things seemed difficult. I hope it inspires you to make the journey too and helps you to keep going to achieve your potential.

When I look back at how things could have been if I had taken the 'sensible option' of accepting a job rather than growing a business:

There's nothing worse than an OK life

Coming in to land

Pilots love their checklists, here's a reminder of important things to be done ...

Planning

Whilst a business plan can show some exciting figures, reality may be different so you may want to change your initial plan to take account of these. This is an obvious point you may think, but so often missed by people – many of whom incidentally don't even have a business plan of any description. It doesn't need to be something prepared only for a bank; it can be for your own use.

Studies have shown that people with plans that have been written down are much more successful than those who haven't bothered. If lists and Excel spreadsheets aren't your thing, at the very least try Mind Mapping your aims and objectives with [coloured] pencil and paper.

There are a few other things you may want to consider in your plan. Again these are all very straightforward but so often forgotten:

i) Having to work maybe double the hours you used to as an employee, at least in the early stages, to cover all the tasks you did not realise were involved in the change from employee to self employed.

ii) Initial client growth may be less than half of your projections - it takes time to build up a reputation and a client base when you first start. The business growth will increase over time but be prepared for the initial stages.

iii) Initial costs may be more than double your projections, as you may be surprised by all the additional expenses that arise when running a business that you didn't account for. If you don't end up spending it, see it as a bonus. If it is factored into your forecasts, it will give you room to breathe or to invest in some 'nice-to-haves'.

Take action
Whilst planning is important there comes a time when you have to make your move and 'burn your boats' to commit yourself to your goals.

There are many people who have great plans but unless they are actioned upon then they don't actually have any value unfortunately.

You are better to get going with a plan that is 80% completed than wait maybe another year to get things up to 90%, as by then some of your market assumptions may need to be revised anyway or a competitor could have launched your product before you. Seth Godin blogged about this recently and I very much agree with him.

Get help
Don't think you can always 'save money' by doing things yourself.

The time, hassle and worry that a professional can save you is well worth the expense – particularly when you consider the value of your own time, and when you should be earning money for the business instead at a much higher value.

There are also communities out there full of like minded people who have been through what you have and are willing to share - I personally recommend Ecademy and BNI as I have a lot of experience with those organisations.

I spent the first couple of years running my business alone struggling to find out things myself and made some mistakes initially trying to 'save money' – *you don't have to.*

Have fun!
Why did you become self employed? You need to know what you are trying to achieve, particularly in the early years when things may be tough. Keeping this in mind will help you to keep going.

What's the most important asset in your business? YOU, so make sure that you book time in your diary for yourself - it can be too easy to get tied up in your work and find that weeks or months have passed without you taking any time off.

For me, one of the reasons I became self employed was so that I had the flexibility to work at the weekend and then take time midweek to go flying. In the early stages, I made the mistake of spending too much time working though. You need to include time for yourself to recharge. In the overall scheme of things booking a few hours a week for personal time won't cost much and will actually increase your productivity.

Exit strategy
Why do you need one of these when you've only just started?

This is an important goal to be aiming towards; the goal should be to add value to your business so that it can generate income even when you are not there and also so that it has a sale value should you wish to pass it on to someone else.

Many self employed people develop a business over many years that only generates income when they are actually there in person. In effect it's just another job but working for themselves instead of someone else. As Michael Gerber states, you've become your own employee and may not like the boss!

This is where the web can also help; maybe you can develop additional products - maybe eBooks about your professional experience in your field or other items that can be sold online.

The costs for electronic distribution are virtually nil so the profit margin is very high on these. You could find that when you wake up in the morning you have actually made money while you slept! These products generate passive income which, in time, can also augment or even become your pension.

About the author

James McBrearty is the CEO of taxhelp.uk.com, a company specialising in helping self employed people pay less tax and avoid fines.

He has grown the company from scratch and experienced himself the challenges that the typical self employed sole trader will inevitably encounter.

James is also an Assistant Director for BNI, as well as being a member himself in his local Esher & Cobham chapter. He regularly trains BNI members both in the UK and internationally.

James has been a qualified private pilot since August 2000 and currently owns a share in a classic Piper Cherokee aircraft which he flies, whenever possible, from White Waltham airfield in Berkshire.

In addition to building up over three hundred and fifty hours in his logbook, he has been lucky enough to have had some great flying adventures which include qualifying to fly on instruments in clouds and bad weather as well as qualifying to fly at night. He has also flown twenty five different types of aircraft, ranging from very light two seat aircraft up to twin engine aircraft costing in excess of four hundred thousand pounds, as well as also 'flying' several multimillion pound airline flight simulators. He flies regularly in the UK and has also flown internationally in

France, Spain, Morocco, Gibraltar and also Nevada and Arizona in the USA.

His core process is 'Achieving Freedom' and his goal is to help people achieve their own freedom.

To find out more about the Core Process, visit Nick Heap's website at www.theflameinstitute.com

Resources

You can find and join with me online at:

Twitter: @taxhelpukcom

Company website: taxhelp.uk.com

Ecademy: ecademy.com/user/jamesmcbrearty

LinkedIn: uk.linkedin.com/in/taxhelpukcom

Facebook: facebook.com/james.mcbrearty

Wordpress blog: taxhelpukcom.wordpress.com

YouTube: youtube.com/user/taxhelpukcom

These are the top three books I recommend:

Networking like a Pro by Dr Ivan Misner
Published by Entrepreneur Press on 1 Jan 2010

Know me, Like me, Follow me by Penny Power
Published by Headline Business Plus on 20 Aug 2009

The E Myth revisited by Michael Gerber
Published by HarperCollins, 3rd edition, on 8 Nov 1994

Social Media: a navigator's guide

Twitter

What is twitter?
This new phenomenon is a simple way of connecting with people easily, both existing friends and new contacts, by the sharing of short one hundred and forty character messages.

One advantage of twitter is that you are limited to the size of a standard text message, which means that it is quick to use as you do not have to spend large amounts of time composing text.

Another key advantage of twitter is that you can include links to other web locations and articles within the message, rather than try to condense what you are saying into a short message.

Quite often I will see a blog or article on the web that is of interest to people and I will send out a short message saying why I like it and providing the link so that people can access it directly.

With the one hundred and forty character limit there are many services online that can shorten links into a few characters so that you are not using up the whole message with the web address.

To learn about its history and how to use it the smart way, I can recommend you buy 140 Characters: The Short Form by one of Twitter's founders, Dom Sagolla. It's available in print but the iPhone version is much more fun as everything he refers to is hyperlinked to the source. This even means you can connect directly with people he talks about as you can from the e-version of this book,

Why bother?
The jumbo jet size business which is Dell Computer has made over three *million* dollars directly attributable to Twitter.

It is a quick and easy way to make connections with people and also to share information.

Many websites now have a share button, such as at the bottom of my homepage taxhelp.uk.com – by including these on your website people are able to share your site very easily with a couple of mouse clicks, rather than having to copy the web address and then paste it into an email for example.

By creating content online, that has *value* to people following you, you are creating greater interest in what you do and from that you will find that as a result people will want to find out more and the hits on your website will increase over time.

You do have to ensure that you are providing information that is of interest and not just a different version of spam, where you constantly just try to get people to look at your site and don't engage in conversations.

Terminology

You will hear various terms mentioned to do with Twitter; the main ones are below and fairly simple to understand.

- 'Tweet' – this is like talking in open networking, it goes to all your friends *and the web*

- 'ReTweet' (RT) – telling your friends *(and the web)* something you heard from someone else

- 'Direct Message' (DM) – talking to someone in private

- #Hashtag - a way of defining a searchable and indexable term that relates to you, your expertise, your interest or products or services

Oddly enough, this manner of communication is exactly how pilots communicate which each other and with ground control. For example, if I spot a bad bit of turbulence, I will pass it on to local aircraft or control towers and they can warn others in advance. Amateur radio enthusiasts do something similar on the ground.

Note that tweets and retweets are shared with the web and that they can be found by anyone who happens to be using a search term that is contained within your message. This is also a powerful way to use twitter as you can search for key words that are of interest to you and then connect with people using them.

If you keep your tweets to less than 100 characters, they can be easily retweeted by at least two other people. The retweet is powerful for two reasons. Firstly, your tweet is rebroadcast to other peoples' followers. Secondly, as someone else is recommending you, it can come with more gravitas and authority.

The scope of the message can be easily seen. A while ago, when I had around ten thousand followers on Twitter I used a web service to measure my second order following. This is the number of people your message would be seen by, if every one of your followers retweeted it. I was amazed to find that, for my @taxhelpukcom account, that number was actually over thirty *million*!

Also as Twitter search is real time you will get answers most closely related to what you are looking for. Whereas a web search may bring up articles and comments from months or years ago, a twitter search will bring up what people are talking about *now* which may only be minutes old.

First Steps
Here are the simple steps to get started with an account on twitter:

1)   Go to twitter.com and register for an account

2)   Search for people that you know and connect with them

3)   See who they follow and if they are relevant then follow them too

4)   Set up access on your mobile device – iPhones and Blackberries are particularly easy with good apps available for download

5)   Download Tweetdeck for free on your computer, or an equivalent desktop program – it makes managing your account much easier

6)   **Regularly update** – at least once a day. I tend to update at least 5-10 times a day.

The last point is very important, so many people say 'I'm on Twitter' or 'I have a Twitter account' but unless you are updating at least once a day on average you really don't actually have an effective account. When potential followers look at your twitter page they will look at the last time you updated to see if you are someone worth following. If you haven't updated for several months then they are unlikely to want to follow you.

How to use it effectively
For me I follow a process described by Penny Power, which is:

"Know me > Like me > Follow me"

You have to generate content for people first to have a chance for them to know you, which is your visibility. Creating content regularly will mean there is a greater chance of people reaching this stage.

From then the process is whether they will like you, or be interested in what you are saying. If you just keep repeating the same message as a type of spam then people are unlikely to. However if you are generating useful content and linking to useful information then they may do.

The final stage is whether they will follow you, or in other terms whether they will be willing to do business with you. This is the last stage of the process and *can't be rushed* – you have to go through the other stages before you reach the stage of doing business.

As to what I tweet about, when I started I may have been using twenty five percent business, twenty five percent social and half making connections by conversing with people. Again, it is not always just about business – people do business with *people.*

An example of this is one of the new clients that came through Twitter – not because of something tax related that I tweeted about; this was simply because a conversation had been started when I asked for film recommendations.

I don't have a rigid set of rules that says I only tweet in these proportions – it is me posting the messages on the account so I will respond as I see fit. It is very much up to the individual as to how they use twitter, this is a guideline but there are no set rules apart from spamming.

Spamming, or 'chumming' as I heard Nick Tadd describe it is where people send you repeated impersonal sales messages. The great thing with twitter is that it is easily dealt with, offenders can be blocked and you won't be contacted by them again.

Recommended Twitterers

Incidentally all the people I have mentioned in this book can be followed on Twitter at:

Ivan Misner	@ivanmisner
Thomas Power	@thomaspower
Penny Power	@pennypower
Nick Tadd	@nicktadd
Vanessa Warwick	@4_walls
Tony Robbins	@tonyrobbins
Seth Godin	@sethgodin
Tom Evans	@thebookwright
Mark Lee	@bookmarklee
Richard White	@richard_white

Facebook

Twitter is very easy to pick up and get started with as the limits to the service actually make it simple to get your head around quickly. Facebook is more advanced, with more options available for sharing.

I tend to use Facebook at present for mainly personal usage, such as sharing my personal photo albums. One of the great advantages with Facebook is the depth you can go into - with Twitter you are limited to a short message of 140 characters to tell people what you are doing, whereas on Facebook there are no such restrictions.

When you post a link on Facebook, it is easy to share this amongst your contacts, and the links are more visual in their display on the service, with embedded videos for example.

Through Facebook I have actually picked up a couple of new clients, even though to date I have not devoted much time to it as my main focus tends to be on Ecademy and Twitter.

There are good opportunities through Facebook due to its size. A few facts about Facebook that may surprise you, from data compiled by website-monitoring.com in early 2010:

1) Facebook has about half a billion users worldwide.
2) If Facebook was a country it would be ranked third in the world.
3) 50% of active users log in every day.
4) The average user spends nearly an hour every day on the site.

Indeed, with the recent release of 'the Facebook movie' and with these sorts of numbers I can see that Facebook is going to increasingly become a part of many people's lives.

Interestingly, the fastest growing age group of users is those between thirty five and sixty five years old.

In 2011, intend to develop my knowledge of the site and to share this in my second book, which will go into the practical steps of using social media sites on a day to day basis, and how to integrate them into your life.

For me, this is like taking my plane into an area I've not been before. My plan is to make sure I've got a good map and that I speak to some people who've been there before me.

LinkedIn

LinkedIn is another site, similar to Facebook, which I have used for some time but not truly explored yet.

I tend to find that it has a more corporate feel to it, which reminds me of the CSC nature of business I have experienced in the past.

The user profile on LinkedIn resembles an online resume or CV and details people's business titles and experience through their career. Some people say it's networking for people looking for their next job placement.

I have a completed profile on the site, and have several clients who communicate regularly with me using LinkedIn messages though. There are also some really useful specialist groups you can communicate and collaborate in.

I have also configured the site so that when I update my Twitter status this feeds through and updates my LinkedIn status. Through this I have had several interesting conversations with contacts, on items that started as a tweet but they responded on LinkedIn and we continued the conversation there.

Due to the numbers of people using LinkedIn, and the fact that it is a business site, it is something I intend to devote some more 'flying time' to in the future in order to investigate the possibilities.

Ecademy

This is my 'home' on the web, it is the site I initially learnt about social media on and it is the site that I have spent most time on.

You may not know that Ecademy was founded in 1998 and predates all the other social media sites – it really is a pioneer. When it was founded, there were no navigational aids and no beacons, just intrepid explorers similar to Amelia Earhart and Charles Lindbergh.

The majority of people on Ecademy seem to be self employed individuals, and that is one of the reasons I feel comfortable there. We have all been or are going through the same situations as each other and that enables us to connect on a deeper level.

The blog section of the site contains many interesting posts daily, on both social and business topics. It was where I first started to blog myself, and the supportive nature of the members there enabled me to develop my skills over time without the negativity that can exist on some other sites - when newcomers are not made to feel as welcome as they should be.

My Ecademy profile was where I first started to embrace the open, random and supportive attitude by sharing personal details. When I came from the corporate world this wasn't something you did, as your identity was synonymous with that of the company.

As I mentioned earlier, our biggest client to date came through Ecademy – and what attracted him to make contact was the personal information in my blog.

Ecademy is constantly developing and the site continues to add extra functionality. They have recently also added an iPhone app that is unique in that it learns about what data feeds are of interest to you and then delivers a customised experience. It's like an electronic sixth sense and is indeed designed by a company called My6Sense.

One of the benefits of my BlackStar membership is the SEO advantages for my profiles, both my personal and my company one. As well as this there are also adverts that can be placed in the marketplace, and an events section.

The power of the SEO is apparent here as well. Recently I was asked if I would like a stand at a local retirement fair held at a racecourse. This was a fairly large event, with many stands, yet was not promoted well on social media. I was impressed when someone came up to my stand and told me the only thing he could find anywhere on the web about the event was my Ecademy event listing! It had taken me all of a few minutes to create this and send it to Twitter as well.

As well as the online benefits of Ecademy, I have also made great connections through the local meetings. The great thing with the site is that you can access delegate lists for these and easily link back to peoples profiles to find out more about them – either before the event in preparation or afterwards if there is someone you want to follow up.
Most people on the site have a profile picture uploaded so finding someone is much easier if you may have not had a chance to speak to them in person before.

Ecademy is definitely my number one recommendation for the social media site you should be on if you want to mix with like minded business people.

There are so many people there that are open and are looking to help you. You can find no end of free advice by posting questions in the various specialist interest groups. As well as a huge amount of suppliers of many diverse services, you will also find people you can collaborate with to deliver new synthesised services.

By far the best use of sites like Ecademy is to build up your advocacy base. In time and just like with BNI, this means you can even stop wasting time on conventional sales and marketing. Your network will bring in all the business you will ever need.

Foursquare

Foursquare is a great example of the new type of location based service that is currently emerging.

The idea with Foursquare is that you 'check in' to locations so that you can connect with people nearby.

For example, you may want to meet up with a group of friends after a conference – using Foursquare you would see where they were from their check in and then join them.

The service is accessed through an app downloaded to your cell phone, which uses the GPS in your phone to find nearby venues that you check in to. You can also add venues to the system yourself, if no one has been there before.

One of the big advantages with this service is the opportunity is presents for business to engage with customers in real time.

Someone may check in to your business and you can offer them a special deal for doing this, such as a discount.

The benefit to the business is that it then has data on their customers, while the customer receives a benefit of a special offer too. It can also be used as a type of loyalty card by recording check ins and rewarding the person who visits the most, which is called the mayor in foursquare. Another benefit for the business is the free publicity it generates for them, as many people link their Foursquare account to their Twitter and Facebook status updates.

These services are just emerging at the moment, and we are just starting to see large business using them now.

Again, as I have found many times, sharing personal information leads to business being done.

I checked in to White Waltham airfield one day when I was going flying and then received a message later from someone looking for tax advice!

They had seen my check in, and it lead them through to my profile which explained what I do.

It will be interesting to see how these services develop, although there is one caveat though – you may not want to share your location freely all the time. For example checking in to a beach on the other side of the world is not the best idea when it also advertises the fact that your home may be empty.

There is an option to go 'off the grid' though and whilst your location isn't then openly shared you will still receive the benefit from any special offers locally.

Blog Example 1 – Business Blog

A quick and easy way to boost a business

I am regularly travelling both domestically and internationally - running seminars for BNI, for my own business and also privately. As I am a heavy user of social networking and the web, one of the things I need is 24/7 Internet access to stay in touch.

I take various devices with me when travelling - my BlackBerry, my 3G Netbook and my iPod Touch and have to juggle them to get the best connection and access.

In the UK, I am surprised about the number of places that don't have wifi or a 3G mobile phone signal. Frequently when travelling I am left with only a basic GPRS mobile connection, which is more than five times slower than dial up used to be! When it is available, there are also many hotels and conference venues that charge up to ten pounds a day for wifi access, and I have found that the quality of connection is not very good anyway.

When you are restricted to this level of connection speed it is surprising how much your experience is affected. Whilst I can still easily access twitter, foursquare, Facebook and email via apps on my BlackBerry, everything else is painfully slow and I usually have to turn off pictures and wait a long time just to download a webpage. Unfortunately this also means I cannot access YouTube or video blogs until I am back in an area of good coverage.

Similarly, I have a series of videos on my website that explain the service and process - if someone was accessing my site through a basic connection then they would lose the benefit of these. Many sites also include extra features that become unavailable when used on mobile devices.

There is a vast difference in experience depending on where I stay and, surprisingly, one of the countries that has the best experience and supply is actually one that people would not associate as being ahead of the UK - Spain.

Also, whilst in the US one of the hotels I stayed at had a great example of how to provide a good signal - they actually had a wifi router inside every room, ensuring that a quality signal was available to all guests. And it was free - are you listening hotel managers out there?

(On a related note Vanessa Warwick recently blogged about how the maximum broadband speed you can achieve in a residential property is now actually starting to affect the house's value, and I'm sure this will only increase in importance with more people working from home.)

Some business people in the UK are however starting to realise that providing a reliable, fast Internet connection is actually a great benefit to them. For example hotels can find that people upload their holiday pictures to Facebook while they are still away - increasing the hotels exposure and allowing people to connect while they are still there.

I was in Guernsey at the weekend and enjoyed a great lunch in a local cafe bar. I was able to connect through Twitter and Foursquare using the mobile signal. If they had wifi for customers then I could have shared more and perhaps even uploaded a short video of the live music playing in the bar - bringing attention to them and they would then have a greater chance of bringing in both returning and new customers.

Businesses that embrace the web and provide services to their guests, without trying to charge for everything, will benefit. Another example happened to me at the weekend - I stayed at the Portland Heights Hotel overnight and received an email on my Blackberry that needed printing. They share the reception's email address freely, so I forwarded the email to them and asked if there was any way I could get a print. I was surprised to receive a message on my phone while I was having dinner to say it had already been printed and was waiting at reception!

This level of service really differentiates them from the competition, where some hotels would direct you to their business centre which is only open in business hours, and would have been charged for too.

When I travel to Spain, both to present BNI training seminars to local chapters and on holiday, the experience there is completely different to most places in the UK. Not only is there a full 3G signal available in most of the coastal areas, there is also free wifi in several public places - a great example is in Orange Square in Marbella.

The cost to the local council of providing this is not much, however as well as providing a service to travellers enabling them to share their experiences it also brings people into the town square where they are most likely to buy a drink, a snack, or even a meal whilst they are connected there. This benefits the local economy directly.

If you take a walk along the seafront in Marbella you will also see signs in most of the bars and restaurants telling people about their free wifi. They have realised that people travelling nowadays will want good web access, and they are directly increasing their trade as a result as well.

Using mobile devices to access the web is forecast to increase massively in the future - I actually already use my iPod Touch most for web access when I'm in a wifi area as it is so quick and easy. If you are watching a TV programme for example you can wake the iTouch up and Google something in only a few seconds, giving you the answer instantly. Alternatively, you can look up a website from an advert straightaway.

With the continuing introduction of new mobile web devices and introduction of the iPad and introduction of other tablet devices, there is a great opportunity for businesses and telecoms operators to provide free and fast web access through both the provision of local wifi and better 3G coverage, which can in turn generate both direct business and publicity for low cost.

Blog Example 2 - Personal Blog

Portmeirion – what's that?
Portmeirion is an amazing place, and somewhere that many people may not realise exists in the UK.

Portmeirion describes itself as "... a private village resort on the coast of Snowdonia".

It was built from 1925 to 1976 by architect Clough William-Ellis in a variety of architectural styles. Surrounding the village are seventy acres of sub-tropical woodland gardens. The site is designated a conservation area and the cottages are listed buildings."

The Prisoner
People may be familiar with the location from the classic 1960's TV series 'The Prisoner' which starred the late Patrick McGoohan as a man who resigns from his top secret job and is held captive in 'The Village' and known only as 'Number six.'

Mensa at Portmeirion 2010
Having been a long term member of Mensa, I was delighted to receive a last minute invitation to attend their 2010 annual gathering at Portmeirion, held over the weekend.

Unfortunately, it clashed with a seminar I was really looking forward to, run by International presenter and fellow BNI director Mark Rhodes. As I was seeing all the presenters in a few weeks time at the BNI European directors' conference, and this was a very special invitation, I decided to attend.

What makes the Mensa gathering special is that they take over most of the cottages in the village meaning that the vast majority of residents are Mensa members for the weekend.

Being a resident means that you are staying within the village and have access when the public are not there - which meant I could take some amazing pictures in the early morning before it opened to visitors.

More information
The village has an excellent website at:

www.portmeirion-village.com

taxhelp.uk.com

taxhelp.uk.com is James McBrearty's company and it specialises in helping self employed people pay less tax and avoid fines.

It offers unique affordable packages, specifically designed to help the self employed sole trader make an easy decision to get help with their tax, rather than struggle on their own.

Many people think they are saving money by doing their own tax, but forget to account for the value of their own time and may also not be claiming for everything that they are entitled to, and could be overpaying tax.

At the time of writing the fixed fee packages are:

£245 bronze service – which provides the accounts and the personal tax return, and is completed from summary details provided by the client, such as a spreadsheet.

£345 silver service – as for the bronze service, this also includes bookkeeping so instead of the summary spreadsheet the client simply hands over the paperwork for processing.

£695+ gold service – this is for special cases with more complex tax affairs, such as people with several businesses or multiple rental properties.

Of course the fees for these services are also an allowable business expense and qualify for tax relief in the accounts, making them even more affordable. Receiving tax relief for advice helping you to pay less tax is always of great interest to clients.

The service makes it easy for people to get help with their tax and take away the worry as appointments can be made at a time and place to suit the client – rather than them have to take time away from their business to travel to the office. There are also several appointments available in the evenings and at the weekends to make it even easier.

People are often concerned about asking questions in case they receive a bill for the time - by offering fixed fees that include queries on the return as part of the package, clients can be reassured about this and any questions can be answered quickly to put their mind at rest.

The reason taxhelp.uk.com are able to keep the fees so reasonable is because of the high levels of referrals they receive from clients; the happier the clients are, the more likely those clients are to recommend taxhelp.uk.com's services.

CPSIA information can be obtained at www.ICGtesting.com
Printed in the USA
LVOW101202020313

322407LV00007B/163/P